T0170931

METAPHYSICAL LICKS

Gregoire Pam Dick

BookThug 2014

bitlit

A **bundled** eBook edition is available
with the purchase of this print book.

CLEARLY PRINT YOUR NAME ABOVE IN UPPER CASE

Instructions to claim your eBook edition:
1. Download the BitLit app for Android or iOS
2. Write your name in **UPPER CASE** above
3. Use the BitLit app to submit a photo
4. Download your eBook to any device

LIBRARY AND ARCHIVES CANADA
CATALOGUING IN PUBLICATION

Dick, Pam, 1963–, author
        Metaphysical licks / Gregoire Pam Dick.

Poems.
Issued in print and electronic formats.
ISBN 978-1-77166-055-6 (pbk.).–ISBN 978-1-77166-067-9 (html)

        I. Title.

PS8607.I33M48 2014   C811'.6   C2014-904792-4
                                    C2014-904793-2

PRINTED IN CANADA

METAPHYSICAL LICKS

lick: a short motif, phrase, or solo in music

Untergang (fünfte Fassung)
Über den weißen Weiher
Sind die wilden Vögel fortgezogen.
Am Abend weht von unseren Sternen ein eisiger Wind.

Über unsere Gräber
Beugt such die zerbrochene Stirne der Nacht.
Unter Eichen schaukeln wir auf einem silbernen Kahn.

Immer klingen die weißen Mauern der Stadt.
Unter Dornenbogen
O mein Bruder klimmen wir blinde Zeiger gen Mitternacht.

Downfall (fifth version)
Over the white pond
The wild birds have moved off.
In the evening, an icy wind slants from our stars.

Over our graves
Night's shattered brow lowers.
Under oaks, we rock in a silver boat.

The city's white walls are always ringing.
Under bent thorns
Oh my brother, we blind clockhands clamber towards midnight.

Georg Trakl, tr. Greta Trakl

I. sister or brother

SUPERTWILIGHT
He was lit. She wrote lit. They got lit.

Das Licht ist zweideutig.

Nein, mehrdeutig.

I had a brother named Georg. Ergo I must be Greta. First I chose him.

Q.E.D. vs. acuity. Or missing her cue. Philosophy is unlearning how to.

Then two years later. Maybe three.

Press the sustain petal on the black and blue. Soundplay in the keys. Plus white to gray it. Taste the German *Tastatur* or taste the door. Of the flower. Incest of English and Deutsch: *endlich*. It says Sh. Strings hidden inside the flat smooth body like nerve strands. A connection of brother and sister. There were several. Also brothers. Mostly Victor.

The past and the present have different haircuts, how come his/hers is still so '70s? I mean mine. *I Me Mine* was one song. Meanings mined like a sister. Stop it, Greta. She liked Georg, he was sad and sensitive, his guitar wept gently.

False start, throat-clearing. The strings might be out of tune, need some tightening or loosening. With my brothers. Don't get nervous pondering the future. It's not becoming. Yes it is. Restart the *Lyrik* to forsake it, beat beauty, confession, immediate experience. You could be singular, plural, formal or informal. If you're speaking to your brothers, there's a form that is intimate, let it use you. Suddenly next to me a young woman appeared with a wounded arm. It bled from German into English. The world bled into the book. Had fallen on the concrete. I mean the abstract.

*

THE STREET: HOW IT SMARTS
This one's blank. The nexus barks. I can't remember. Disinterest is

aesthetic, self-interest is prophetic. Ethics of sidewalks. Furthermore pathetic: eyebrows don't lie. Just because the light glows, it doesn't follow that there has to be a metaphor. Perspicuous presentation of my anxiety popsicle. Representation a fad. The words doffed their curves and the meanings fumbled, trembled. Voices behind the door infer places. It's not right, it is flat. Metaphysical placemat. Rhymes punch reasons like sister and brother. The girl was no girl but she remained invisible. Also the outer suckled world mugged me, I mean quick language mugged me. Auto-tongue-lashing program of the first person I-vehicle. Then it bit it. Whips of vagrant shouts. The street goes theory-proof. Balking necks. Elbow directions. Urge like a belt.

INTRODUCTION
This is Victor Trakl. *Guten Tag. Guten Tag.* And this is his sister, Greta. *Tag. Hallo.*

SIBLING CHILDHOOD
They played tag.

INCIDENT
The rubber band leapt off the white circle which, outside the visual field, was a table. Except there is no outside. It was red. Don't be clear or you'll destroy subjectivity. Inwardness will crumple like a thin tent. Tents are for aliens. Aagh, so obvious! Awkward psoriasis! A racy sis. Running away from the body versus the mind. No room for my brother or a bad omen.

INCARNATIONS
Face flushed with shame. Scalp paled with fear.

AWAY!
Away from claustral incursions. The grammatical is fanatical: a mythologizing of paths. The PATH goes to New Jersey, but I refused to switch shirts. Am I now to be Victor?

RELIEF
This feels good: hangnail sketch, awesome cuticle! Hold a word up, close one I. Each soul is automotive, swerving. No shortage of fuel,

i.e. evidence. I feel, therefrom I am.

EVENT
Brother and sister played with colored blocks. Victor built a tower, then he knocked it down. Greta made a low fortress wall or other enclosure. Inside it, she put her blue Keds sneaker. It was a speech ribbon. It was of speech. It could kick if necessary.

ABSTRACTION FROM CHARACTERS
That trick with adjectives and poetical morals. Ironic foils, iron turnstiles. The styles are crucial. It's a transformation when you grasp how many mishits, misdirections. Indirect communication: the lie that does not speak its name. I wrote numb. Didn't mean it. Still, no glow lit up my mentality. The thing is, I must keep on keeping on. Alright, Greta.

NUMSKULL
The crow means decay and ruin's childhood. I dreamt of a pearl gray dove, I held it lossly (sic), it was curved, warm and throbbing. It did not talk because it was no gray parrot. I named it Otto or possibly Olga. These names only name because the bird practiced its commandments. Numskull is not true anymore. Tongues and wings flap. Reminders are for overdue books or nostalgia. That's no way to think. Madness morsels. Flickers of consequents. The ill logic of conditionals.

GRETA TREK ILL
Go on, keep on, keep on going, go on keeping, keep going on, go keeping on, go on ahead, keep heading on, keep to that heading, keep heading ongoing, ongoing head keeping, keep keeping head on, keep your head on. Or *keep* means a fortress. A different game. But I hate the idea of games of the language. I do not wish to play. Immunity boosters in the form of syntactical sidesteps, trips and shuffles. She stepped on some pink gum, it slowed her down. The pavements glinted. Shards of syllables flipped the aspect into something abstract. Don't say it, show it. Greta entailed lines from her eyes' pupils. The radiator's her witness, gnashes its teeth. Heat around the body, the former paragraph refusing to linger. The end of the page beckons like the tenor's *Dichterliebe*. Ghosts journey across

the floral bedroom. Uneven handwriting. The temptation of simple referents. Inability to stop when you want to. All of this was filched from Lukerl's formulas. Girls more than boys are kleptos. But he said Jews. But the muted particulars keep their own counsel: flagrant tune-ups. Mysterious inklings. I will cease before it wilts.

GEARSHIFT
Now, again, uncanny rigor. Repetition's finesse. Or the limits of the free.

QUERY
Does that mean we get to walk through the park again, notice the things? Or only through the book?

*

CHILDHOOD'S RUIN
Something new is needed here. I, Greta, can't remember what. Meanwhile, they're remodeling the other one. They favored symmetry over eccentricity of expression. Voices huddled, nobody bought smoke. Cement rose up in hopeless protest. Childhood head bands, German breadstuffs, amputees on dollies. My intention no entailment. Great fatigue split the votive, it spluttered. Remorse tugs on my hair.

KNOTS
Now I am being bad. Once the mother combed Greta's tangled hair to punish her. Some imperative, or philosophical hygiene! *The connections ball up* is a bad fate. That's what *they* say. But intensions waver. Time for mute shirt buttons. Though the hair could get caught on them, if it were longer. I think you should cut it off. Aka out. *Out* means quit it.

*

NEW PHILOSOPHY
It swallows its words. Time is a maze. Spell of the bramble. The briar's paradox. Greta doesn't sleep from being pricked.

*

SLIGHTLY BLUISH VERY PALE GRAY NOTEBOOK
But still the truth. The world when it's invented.

They say the language doesn't touch but it touches. Like sister and brother.

There is nothing except language. It touches itself. One hand pressed to the other. Or one chest to. Also music is a language.

My brother Ludvik brought me a beautiful olive-toned notebook from the italic war-dressed mountains which were not Alps. He wanted me to live in it. It was austere, minimal, silent like a tower. He obsessed over the stitches, the leather of the cover, the paper. But I wanted to live in my own book, which was slim, flimsy, imperfect. I stole it from the 5-and-10, because girls are kleptos. I stole that thought phrasing from my younger self or paragraph. Although some boys or brothers or friends or lovers who are young men also steal. Mostly thoughts or sentences. Ludvik admitted that he himself did. Do I do it because I am so androgynous?

I went into the kitchen to reheat my philosophy. Each time it tastes more bitter, but I keep reheating it.

It is how to stay awake. Sleeping is death. There exists a fear of it.

Dream of reproaching the negligent father. Antonius?

Then sex with a smooth-skinned shining girl. She said slow down. In a grand hotel in a European capital such as Oslo or Vienna. First the room had to be switched. Or it couldn't be found, or I did not want to live in it with Ludvik. Also I could not slow down, so I felt bad.

My notebook is light gray, the cover is made of thicker paper. The notebook is unruled. It smells like gray philosophy.

Ludvik said, There's nothing left for you to do. Why don't you write music? I said, The lyrics are philosophy. Music is philosophy with truth lyrics and notes of metaphysics.

The truth of the made-up world is as real as the truth of the inflicted world: there's no difference of the substances.

Truth is the form, meaning the content. The world, any world, is made up of meanings.

The truth is the world, I am the truth. I am the world. These equivalences hum in a major or minor key, depending.

The truth has two aspects and two sides: subjectivity and objectivity, veracity and reality. The graph of veridical space has four quadrants. The vertical axis is the I-axis for the first person singular, the horizontal axis is the w-axis for the world.

Going clockwise from the upper left quadrant, there is: objective veracity (thought, proposition), objective reality (fact, thing), subjective reality (my thing), subjective veracity (my thinking, thought). The truth is the graph. The meaning is the graph paper.

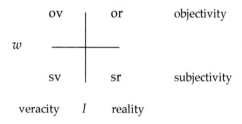

The paper together with the graph is language. I.e. the whole picture. It has parts such as words, phrases, sentences. Phrasing is musical.

The truth is the structure. The meaning is the content.

What is the raw material? Sound?

Isn't the raw material just belief, i.e. faith? Awe material.

They said Greta is *aggressive, hysterical and pathologically eccentric*. I mean Grete. I mean now I am Greta, but what does that mean?

I used to be rigorous but then I saw that I had to sacrifice myself for the truth, which demanded irrational music and lying prose, a prone pose, waiting for the inspiration to enter my mouth like a brow. My chest like an iron.

*

MELANCHOLY OF BRANCHES
She coughed, he sang,
                 stammered, not stentorian.
Pain from banging
                      the head against the wall.
Mortification or accident.
To put to death the other projects.
My brother stole something.
What?
His name was—
Do not do that.
Or too close: incest of homophones.
I don't know if I can go
                 on with this, says she.
Gregoire?
Ugliness of arms in the sun.
Light the form of judgment.
Lost faculties.
Or loaded whiteness
                 into the vehicle backwards.
Mortification of accident.
The mother's voice.
This machine not mimetic, rather stony
                      or fluid.
Pale spring green of hospital.
But the girl can't cure anybody.
Alone on a threshold, watching masks.
Their voices rise like trash, the
                    trees lie.
Black shroud on building.
I don't care if this is
             hopeless.
I favor it, vows Gregoire.

THE BROTHER BLOCKED THE PATH
The sister stops.
There exist other paths.
But she is stubborn.

THE SIBLINGS ARE CALLED TRAKL
Greta, her brother Georg, her brother Victor, her brother Haakon, her
brother Gregor, her brother Ludvig (aka Ludvik, Lukerl).
The girl had five brothers, as in a fairy tale.
The flower is not blue.
Yes it is.
The flower is a boy flower.
The girl is a boy
                           flower, like her brothers. But
                                                           different.
Therefore the flower is yellow. Therefore the flower is
                                                           not blue.
The father's name is Antoine, but he is like a brother, therefore
Antonius as if Gregorius.
The girl has six brothers, as in a fantasy.
He was erroneously associated with a flower.
Then she lost her petals.
Later it was spring. Later my head hurts.
                                              Bursts?
When meaning and truth are brother and sister.
I thought faith and truth were.
Then faith lost its petals.
The cliché of the flower in a poem. I don't
                                              care.
Or she wants to die, be plucked and pressed flat in a book.
Vow his
           flatness. Or his cold metallic look.
Like this machine. Or her flatness
                                        of affect.
The people rejoice with the coming of spring.
Up here, she clings to her ice cliff, it is red-faced.
Red. Yellow. Black. Green.
Stay away from brown, blue, silver.
What if unable?

From crimson, yes. Maybe.
You should not stroke Georg's words like this.
But a sister.
The siblings.
Broken off.

COMMANDMENT
Oblique the story.

CLOSET QUA HEAVEN
Seven minutes in.
Teach the brother or let the brother teach you.
Brother means boy.

MYSTERY
Change the story.
The story changes itself.
Contradictions versus indirection.
The figure of the story appears at twilight.
You run away from it.

CONFESSION
It is not true anyway.

*

LIGHT GRAY FAINTLY BLUE NOTEBOOK
Grete played the piano, I don't know yet if Greta does. How I wish
that she would play it!

Greta hits notes that are philosophy.

The desire to uphold or deny reference rests on a confusion.

The reference is the set of all senses / modes of presentation.
Denotation.

The inferences are also senses, but are modes of implication,
intimation. Connotation.

Denotation and connotation both made of notes!

Formally, the first person rules over everything. But it is invaded by other views i.e. voices.

There is an I, but is it free? What is freedom? Is it immature to ask that?

The first person singular includes subjectivity, but also objectivity. The transcendental biject. Or I-ject?

They said, Greta is bisexual.

My brother Georg tried to remove his I, thereby to be abstract, objective, but I said, Dear brother, your I is still implicit. It need not be said: it shows itself. The truth is always first-personal. He whispered, I do not wish to be a person. Greta stroked his long wiry blond hair or his cropped wiry blond hair, depending on the fourth-dimensional context.

When I go to Berlin, I will take my five brilliant brothers with me. I mean they'll visit my mentality. Also my one savvy sister-in-law Lola, my brother Haakon's shameless wife. They are in my world, thus mine!

They said, You are thrown into the world, it speaks you; I retorted, The world is thrown out of me, I speak it. At the origin, the world and the I contract to one, a point. The mystical.

Then is the transcendental I also the object, not only the subject? The world, not only the first person? So the world, too, is transcendental?

The mystery of solipsism. My brother Ludvig couldn't solve it.

The Isolate Paradox!

The world I am thrown into is always already the world for me. The first person singular world. No escape from my experience.

If I could only sit up straighter, my thoughts would be clearer.

My training bra is cutting into my ribs like that crucifixion wound.

Georg, I miss you. I am suddenly tired of playing with Lukerl.

But Haakon was playing with Georg. Greta wondered what he was doing with him. She felt lonely. As lonely as Gregor, who was missing. Should she seek out Victor?

Thoughts of Victor who could be like this or like that. Different ways to be the brother.

The day as halting stuttered. Greta drank liquids. Light moved out of the way. Didn't care.

*

Fraction vs. Infraction
Mistake of idle rhyming. Evening aphorism of the buzz saw. Incomplete is something else and worth a pamphlet. Anton Webern's earplugs. To try to extricate myself from the logic contraption of before-it's-too-late. Romantic totality conniption. Or be affectless and impassive of the face. *I have a rendezvous with the Deity.* But the expression a fortification: skin of a double negation. Or infinite by sonic curtains. Let them eat fakes. Let me eat flakes. A noble's title: the not-imperative. Then childhoods clattered below these meditations. Next one is the world. Solve the system of equations for x. Or scratch the system. Loose connections crackle if they don't pop. No absolute certainty. Instead, vulnerability tablets. With metaphysical coatings. And the question of depiction. What divides what? What subtracts what? What adds what? What's a multiplied table?

I Think I Understand Now
But it is really dark in here. Also, I am hungry.

Webster's Catatonic Secret Mission
Schizophrenic stupor, negativism, rigidity, purposeless excitement and abnormal posturing. My brother Georg Trakl as a drugstore clerk.

I Blew It
I blew it.

Asymmetry
Where is the old fountain?

At Stake
If I leave, I shall not return.

*

Station
At the new pen. Or shifted, locked field hospital. No supplies. Gone
for so long. Unpolished crack-up. Supposed to learn how to say
suffering. Instead reflexive action verb. Georg's comrades stopped
him. Who will be my comrades? In the psychiatric clinic. Further
observation. *Gregoire* means watchful, *Georg* means tiller. I was
Gregoire unless Mina. Or Greta, a girl. Thrust in like a long tongue.
It distorts the shape of that makeshift language. Then the words
piled in, they needed me to attend to them, they were wounded.
Harrowing experience of the aftermath of the battle of Grodek. After
math, a different foreign language, e.g. German. Its music. An older
teacher/private tutor named Markus, which implies Tristan. I'll
teach you with song lyrics as if from some curt opera. Three pens:
father, son, holy sister. A Trakl opera? Or Webern's young songs.
It was three days until they buried him. But he is no evidence of a
universality. Though she also did cocaine—vs. sleeping pills. *Till*
means until as in fight till death. Or before. Also strive after, get,
develop, cultivate. Like *Bildung* or *Bildungsroman* or *Bildungslyrik*. Or
Unbildungsroman or *Unbildungsnovelle*. The building across the street
is acquiring a blood-red zipped-tight sweatshirt. Earlier, I pretended
that red did not exist. Then his sister Grete coughed some up. Or
my skull leaked. Will Greta and Victor still exist, so many weeks
after falling silent? The words led everywhere, a field of magnetism.
Field, *Feld*, felled, felt. *Art is the expression of reality as felt.* The Ab Ex
stamps saved us yesterday. Before that, this was dying. Even already
dead. Furrowed? Once Georg ploughed the soiled. But till is also
sprout, stalk. Especially from the lower or base part. Motif of plants,
because it's spring. Like being 26, only you feel older. Or 16, a girl's

party, all the songs about deflowering. Or 36, only you feel younger. High-pitched youth culture of the throat. Re *Bildung*: rebuilding discourses! Guitar licks. That's why they call me a young man. Proof me when I try to enter the electronic music, buy coke. I mean vodka. Krakow. Those two Poles were the first poets I fell in love with, so I was bipolar! Also how I got included in that task/homework. Why couldn't I be learning that? I want to be learning that! Because in fact, they hate you. It all spilled out so easily like blood! I decided to bleed to death on this manuscript, I started with a paper cut. If you position it correctly on your wrist, it works. The myth of self-expression. The myth of no self-expression. Being a consciousness doesn't mean saying *I think* but it means some I is thinking. Where thinking = feeling, dreading, believing, wanting, etc. But the I is just active awareness, not a fixed character like some letter or the letter you could write to your brother, a brief. But *farmer/Georg* comes from fix, make firm. Yet also from lease, rent. As in: she rented his poem, then it rent her. Or raising corps I mean corpse I mean crops I mean cropped hair because he joined up as an orderly but was all alone tending to their suffering and could not, could not. Because it hurts too much because of suffering. Georg is a tiller who's soiled and infirm, and land is goth like *Twilight* but akin to church and to enclosure but you can't be or remain enclosed because of all the suffering, so then how can you be a church? Spiritual adjectival questions as of wandering, homeless, exiled, unlanded. Or crash landing. Or I'm crashing. The Medical Corps. The corpus of work such as writing. It's meditating on the mind/body. And brother Lukerl. Further the question of the will. Also of being in the military, like the uniforms I had in high school. After math. After myth. After meth. Dead or dying. Or confined against his will. People think that I am 27 like Georg. *Fearful of being sentenced to death by Court Martial and increasingly suffering from depression.* Georg fled to death.

*

VERY LIGHT GRAY-BLUE NOTEBOOK
Into my brother's mirror. Georg's vs. Ludvig's.

If the sister could quit imitating, could instead express. How your nightlight turns the world into you. The world is the mirror. The world is the I.

Therefore solipsism was a candle flame that licked. It burned up everything. So she is a pyro?

I am my room. The whole world is my room.

I don't want to understand the symbols!

My brother Ludvik said training, use.

My brother Georg said expression, voice.

Or did I, the sister, say it?

Pictorial bad manners. Rival picture theories. One was projection. How brothers like to watch. And to pin down the impressionable sister. But I don't want to be pinned down. Because I like to roam. The I hyperactive, the mind active! A Plotinus projector whirs in the darkened room. Sometimes it gets stuck.

The radiance. Radiating out. Into the brother's dark world. He held your wrist like a flashlight.

Narcissus, forgetting his solipsism, falls in love with his projection.

But it scares me how I can't get out.

Georg's hard where, Greta's wet where. Then the inverse.

Also the fountain, motif of water. Of her pond. I don't want to be a statue!

That the world is *my* creation.

It's the question of how words mean. And what.

Mystical correspondence vs. passive reception vs. active invention. Or being mutual like doing 69 or being entered or being aggressive, thrusting out.

But if the language could be freed from things, pictures, intentions? Could be pure like music?

Are the Chinese symbols dead or are they glowing? Their ardent gorgeous strokes.

Another reality vs. no reality?

The *life* comes from the feeling, the expression. Which is flowing out of you.

The mirror was a fantasy. The stage of the mirror was also a fantasy. It's taste, touch, hearing that give the *one* world, the fused all or everything.

Jis fusion!

How the sounds might resurrect the world. The notes, the tones might.

But these sounds: don't they also come from you? So the room is still containing you?

Is it bad to stay alone in your room?

Or do the sounds simply come *through* you?

The flowing subject!

*

LIMITS OF MY LANGUAGE

The ideas sat three inches to the left. Fold your arms like cards or sheets with tiny pink flowers. Supernova into vestibule. Strangers thieved the view. Some generator generates. Left eye abraded from trying to improve itself. Stale bars of music. Robert Schumann with some problems. They disappear if you don't look at them. You only look because addicted. A less literal bona fide? Ungrammatical interloper. Still there's some meaning. It could be hidden. Dizzy

recalcitrance. Lapsed path clicks. Lisped pathetics aka comics go
mano-à-mano with Søren's *speculative buskins*. A shout of work! In
the series of teeth. Each item perfect. But bar code head paralysis.
Drowning fits the mood lighting. Thin filaments of regrets meet
altercations in a pawn shop. They used to fix Adam's apples there.
The true son of God walks on words. Maybe in Chinese. Inspecting
the sample won't help. The topic of appearances, i.e. phenomena,
presentations. Philosophy flips a switch, the lightbulb goes on or
it blows. This is my room. I am in my room, so it is not in me. So it
isn't the pure visual room, nor the thought experiment! I am Victor, a
Chinese boy. Unless I am a girl. Injecting the simple won't help.

*

TWILIGHT
Hoping for glossolalia when a shoulder testified. Do this without
reading, use the flourishes of hand jests. To hide the inwardness,
graph a hyperbola. Colored pencils made geometrical reasoning
more convincing. But algebra was Greta's favorite. Victor preferred
Spanish and gym class. Husky men stood around, being different.
All the blood got sucked out of my neck by a guy with eyebrows.
I supplied my own fangs to give him permission. We made a lot
of money. Pale like milk. The crowds adored us. Søren frowned
contemptuously. Trakl lurked in the doorway of the book.
Here comes dusk. The morbid deductions knock out the weird
investigations. Where is my Ludwig Pez dispenser? I don't know
if this will suffice. Pull on the upper lip for a hint. Then blueness
consumed us. No, a floor spill. Skip the decisive ending.

PHRASE
Milk splinters. Ink milk splinters. Dark milk splinters. *Schwärze
Milchsplitter.*

SUBJECTIVE THINKER
About to pass out from the eternal neck wound. God no good at
judging distances, depth perceptions. Young men are spoiled by
their mamas, only Victor wasn't. Thus his wiry limbs admit of
infrastructure. Or delicate notes like Franz Schubert. It's not enough
to do what you do, you have to do what you don't do. So what if
the *Über* living in that building is a fake? Unwarranted assertibility,

inferential nobility. Evidence? Just undo it!

THIS WAS SUPPOSED TO BE ABLE TO GO ANYWHERE
The copy shop lady's son got into a good school, I got an A in that
German class. Indian boys are spoiled by their mamas, whereas
Greta wasn't. Though her artistic mama arranged for Greta's i.e.
Grete's piano lessons. Would have liked her to go a good *Gymnasium*,
but girls aren't allowed. Yes they are—now!—so Greta's mama sent
her. Pull this day out, it hurts from a cavity. The issue of expressions
in semantics presses its face to the window, yielding souls. Goethe
Gerte Grete Greta. Greta switches moods, whips herself like a top,
claims her rod is hot. But the pathetic side of striving keeps cropping
up.

UPS
If we could be united in serving up our parcels, get delivered. Brown
deliverance of monads or consciousness bites. Two-bit coordinates.
Everything perfectly splayed on the graphomatic eiderdown. First
we'd need to have bigger legs, double-park.

HAPLESS
In the room, because outside has spatial expressions of facial
expressions, and Victor is afraid of them. Or else Greta is afraid,
Victor wears two eye patches. His head's not a tumor, so nobody
cares about him, raises money. Nothing makes the propositions into
actions, they stay lying down. Missed that *Wild Child* movie, too.

NOT EVEN
It must be bad. If too good, it's thick like Being, with no possible
holes or motions. The Russian accent on the watch ticks, this guy
thinks he knows something! But life *is* activity. Ergo Plotinus,
Augustine, Ludwig. A consensus of mute gestures. One is thrusting
your obscene tongue out to be inspected. No Pentecost; maybe its
audition. The tone singed the intension while things started to get
silver. Cutting class leads to Catherine Deneuve. Her hunger! The
yellow bookmark went on strike.

CONFESSION #2
I don't *want* to know how to go on.

GEORG'S LAMENT
Unfree. Unfree. Unfree. Unfree. Unfree. Unfree. Unfree.

GRETA'S LAMENT
Unfree, unfree, unfree, unfree, unfree, unfree, unfree, unfree!

*

LIGHT UNLESS MEDIUM BLUE-GRAY NOTEBOOK
Question of the sequence. If it's free. Also its contents, discontents and malcontents.

How the point of view could alter, be altered. But doesn't it come *to* me, not *from* me? Or you are responsible for everything anyway, even if you couldn't have done otherwise. Ardl Sebastian's idea of the *morality* of your character, even though it's your fate? And still the freedom to *say* yes, no? Or to feel it?

The idea of contingency is not the idea of freedom. But what affects what? The question of power.

Perception of freedom merely a sign of ignorance? As says Benek Esteban. Or a sign of will to power—which isn't free! As says Ferdek Thurstan.

Benek was Baruch, a Jew yet a philosopher, and was excommunicated and changed his name to Latin, Benedictus, then was he free?

Then I made him into Polish, it was ironic, also a tic.

The negative notion of freedom vs. the positive. The positive entails, demands the negative. But not the inverse.

He was an ex-Jew, therefore Grete Trakl might not have refused to read him. Anyway, Greta ≠ Grete. Different spells pronounce them. Or how they end. Though both with avowals of disavowels.

If how you end is open, could you decide, will it? By change of name, letter, note?

The question of free will is not academic in a *collected essays* by an ex-preposition such as *for*. The question of self-knowledge is pink and green, the question of meaning is yellow and blue, the question of truth is I can't remember its color.

Uncollected essays as in desperate attempts.

But if all the moments actually already exist, all at once, in a sort of atemporal space, although we can only be at one point at a time?

Incomprehension of the vastness of interconnections. Not strictly causal: logical. Is it possible to become superlogical?

Right now I am wrecked by the illogical disconnectives, hangover of demonstrative *this*. And hair so greasy, it looks raven black as of a druggy fairy tale. Also my tongue grew too big.

*

TYPE IN AROUND PAGE 28
The young champion like Dean or the lanky blond element boy chewing, grinning, hair flopping over brow. Outside smoked. Honesty and the performance of thinking as in feeling. The performance of honesty. It's easier for boys to be passive and vulnerable, because their mamas, sisters, girlfriends, boyfriends will protect them. But prelapsarian crotch shots show equal sensitivity. I left my jeans unzipped to engender pity. Not pity; compassion. Not compassion; tender love. Like Elizabeth Taylor had for Montgomery Clift. Though girls such as Lola don't even like me! Tristan Metro was Chinese on the TV, asking for meaningful work, a former corpsman like Georg, he had not killed himself yet. *Raise High the Roofbeams, Carpenter/Seymour: an Introduction* got big, dusky blue in my father's version. Maybe I prefer the small slender dark ochre one. Hard to be uncovered in the 1950s. Coming of age in the boarding school. Another father such as Laurence taking his brow off. Going too far? The guy's keyboard stops me. A boring girl pays her bills, tainting the collective and potentially mystical thought cloud with loud sky writing. Letters could be white and black stars or Willem's early paintings, but I, Gregoire, neglected to read them. Some second girl won't write me back. Social humiliation performed due

to fatigue that became existential, odorous. She went into the other world to shoot herself. I molded my hair into a bird's crest, pictured being dove gray again. The book could have been held in his elegant hands. Also a cigarette. It's not too bright to go backwards. Greta, 13, ingested Austrian pizza and bagels. Tried to avoid Victor, Georg, Gregor. Ludvik at boarding school when his brothers. No, Grete at music school when her father. Although that's natural, so different. Deviant inference rules. Alien logic of the brothers. Don't know what Boolean logic is, but that logic book by George Boolos was red, bright blue and muscular like Superman. Paying her debts, *then* leaving, vs. paying her debts, *thus* leaving. Question of legible connectives. Brawny white man curled on curb, peeling off his sock to inspect his swollen vagrant foot. Petite Asian lady with girlish black bob and bangs, scavenging bottles. Gregoire Dick's scary scary world. Aching scar on forehead. The one on the back of the head vanished because it was innocent or Franz. The other Franz. Behind me, possible worlds in thick-heeled ladies' boots. Feel cold, thus you know you aren't dead yet. Rereading that book entails leaping into the elevator shaft? A musician fell, Greta's face froze hearing it. Inhumanly, she yawned a micro-abyss. Let the sounds be pink slips, fire this. Letters shrink from sense. Veterans survive wars, like my brother Ludvig, not my brother Georg. Or my brother Victor, not my father Antoine. Should I rename him Grahame? Lately that impulse has pressed into me, I the button, world the elevator—or I am the elevator! Dean said, The world is all that is the staircase—no, the open case!—vs. Ludvik. Dean is like James Dean: confused, sensitive, struggling with words, vulnerable, teenage heartthrob. The audience fell in love with him. Not with Greta's infected paper cut. The back-to-black sickness so heavy. Or hitting the sack with your sexed-up sighing brother. A stranger called me honey; I didn't deserve it. I wear a ripped-up shirt so they won't want me, will disdain me. My shoulder snaps its fingers at me to hurry up. I never heard from that Ken doll again. It's ok, the G.I. Joe was sexier. Tallness squawked. A cup of kawfee. The Koughka, Kawfka, Kopfka proof, its or his formality. Ludvik's formalism. What exactly is formalism? Wearing your hard on your book sleeve, your straight on your jacket? The dialethic deathly one joins the line of customers. Green pallor, long hair but just a few strands left. No eyeballs. The thought of his corpse revolting. Inspiration means he breathes from his mouth into your mouth, resuscitates your death wish. The music doesn't clank with infinity. The man's red crack a flash card, on the other side his prick. X-rated language can't reconnoiter. Husky skepticism, scrawny anxiety. Never a thin enough account of meaning. She liked chewing, hated swallowing. Sexed edit. Please, I would like another now now. Or some different theme prick. But Ludvik lay and tempted her with his Clearasil. Commercials on the teenage channels fondle. Childish treatment of the death theme, it needs another variation, compositional method, interpretation. Do the interpretations of *final* come to an end? Do they compose a rest? Or do they simply keep going?

*

LIGHTER SHADE OF PALE GRAY NOTEBOOK
Consciousness comes after, when something in the body is already happening.

But the body *is* the soul, the spirit. Otherwise a dead thing.

Although an object could be derivatively animated, alive? In a divine gaze? But not the body when it's dead.

Don't keep thinking about his dead body!

Do I have to leave my room? I did not want to be outside, Greta couldn't help it, was I free to stay in my room, yet not be Greta?

If the whole world is my room, then I am not free to leave it.

Claustrophobia of solipsism. Georg's and Greta's fear of the elevator. Also her dream of it, where it goes sideways, a moving cell.

Not: I am all that exists. Rather: all I experience is how it exists *for* me. Even the unknowable is so *for me*. Thus existential, not ontological solipsism? There exist other worlds, for others—but they, too, are part of my world. The unlit part.

This is how solipsism collapses into realism, as says my brother Ludvig?

Or simply because this solipsism, of the metaphysical I or subject at the limit of its world, goes and must go without saying, only with showing? But I reject his abstraction of that I!

But is the most metaphysical connective, while *for* is the most metaphysical preposition—no, *to*! For it has *for*'s meaning, and also crucial others.

But that is idealism, not solipsism! Isn't it the preposition *in* that gets you? Or what gets you? The question of the curse.

But fatalism's always incomplete, disingenuous? If fatalism were complete, the true world would be provable.

And *or*, not *but*, is the most metaphysical connective?

Then a question about systems. How they could be sounds. But the broken connections. The impulses firing haphazardly! A dim sense of infinite connections. Or a dimming. My left flank hurts.

Greta has wrecked her ability to focus, think abstractly, with her sex, her drugs, her rockiness, her sister role.

How they wouldn't let you into the bright words. The boys. Or his face, how it repeated. How her handwriting got bigger yet less legible. How the scores were unsettled. Like stars.

But the question of truth cannot be answered unless the question of will is answered. And every other question.

The world augments or diminishes as a whole, said my brother Ludvik, mimicking our tutor Fedka.

The poetics and metaphysics rise or fall together. Like brother and sister.

But what of the ascendency of the fragment, scrap?

The world is just: all the fragments. The collection of scraps, not of things. But *that's* never a whole. But it rises or falls as one larger scrap. A shred or shard.

Then they destroyed the ground, and it rained, and the glass didn't shatter, and a minute was not a minute, grew much longer.

And the question was where to get another hit, a fix. Where she could be fixed.

Thus not get pregnant, not have the abortion.

For they hunt me *like an animal,* she said.

Or the deer in his poetry. Or the blackbirds.

If I licked all of Georg's imagery, would I feel him again?

*

GRETE FADES IN AND OUT WITH GEORG
His *animal drives* vs. angel apprenticeship, nervous exhaustion, explosion, prick of so-called *howling demon.* Mad flesh transfigured by harmonious music into beautiful pictures. Unreality! In myself, I am my world. The euphonious whole. He said, Grete, play for me! In Vienna, he taught her drugs. She studied theory and composition. Pursued piano with her master Pavel, chased Georg's friend Erhard. My brother shadows me! His early plays have violent love of the sister or some Grete. In Berlin, more piano, chamber music, harmony, until Grete quit because of illness or other stranger conditions. My unhappy brother. Then met a man with a giant head. A decoy, it didn't block Georg, drugs, decay. Grete as the Empath on *Star Trek.* Her face shows his marks.

*

REDO THE EARLY ENDING
...Dead or dying. Or confined against her will. People think that I am 26 like Grete. *Two unsuccessful drug cures and financial crises, combined with the unwillingness or inability of friends to help.* Grete bled to death.

31

FORMALITY
26 or 27? I will be 25 or 28. Different ways to complete the series.
Then the digit, index finger, changed, but it made no difference. Only
in form.

OUTSIDE LOOKING IN
Why out here? The room would be silent, private, sensitive, tender,
bookish, uncontaminated. But fear of the father floating in the corner.
Or the loneliness of mirrors. Yet out here there are windows of
loneliness. Eyes are mouths. The two little kids: older sister, younger
brother. The sister doesn't cover her mouth when she chews.

INDEX
Narcotic wasn't in the index finger. Yes it was, in the pattern of
whorls. The essential indexical fingered me.

OBJECTIVITY OF SUBJECTIVITY
The whorl is all that is the case. The I drops away. Solipsism turns
into realism because they French kiss. Georg fell for Rimbaud.
Season in infer = says I in infirmary. Today my world or I does not
feel well.

SUBJECTIVITY OF OBJECTIVITY
The world is all that is your case. The case against you.

IN HIS POEMS (GRETA OF SOPHIE = PEARL OF WISDOM)
Möndchin = sister or girl monk. Like Edvard Munch's sister Sophie
in Oslo. She was sick and died on him, he blamed their father. Don't
bring that in! But the Oslo leitmotiv: its sex, its snow, its room.

THEIR YOUTH
Grete away at the School of the Unangelic Sisters in Saint Pelts,
Georg flunking out of math and classical language. He a solo druggy,
still drinks with the *spinnertes Grätzl*, the crazy crew. She a solo
prodigy, even by age 7. When home, sat on the swing in the garden,
listened to Mademoiselle's stories, loved Rimbaud all by herself. At
14, she heard her bro's confidences. They swore hi-fi in stereo.

To the Lamppost or the No Parking Sign or the Air
Two kids' bikes chained together. No arms or legs, only torsos: they were wounded. One ivory like a piano key, one violet-blue like a bruise. Grete and Georg.

His Life an Open Shirt
Still tall, homeless, shouting, with his smooth royal purple-black chest showing. *It is shining* was true, so one believer stood under an awning. Some addicts are homeless in life, some are in poems like Georg. Not at home in a home key in a musical composition. This pop music is disgusting. A duo from our preteenhood: *Hölle und Eide*, Hell & Oaths. *You're out of touch, I'm out of time, I'm out of my head when you're not around.* Grete didn't visit Georg.

Berlin
Later he went to see her as she recovered from almost bleeding to death from the miscarriage or messed-up abortion. Maybe it was of a bastardized opera they had composed together. Hypersensitivity. It was called *Family EP*. Or *Night Move*. Or *Astray*. Or *Night Trauma*. Or *Hour of Groans*. Or *Bro and Sis*.

1 or 2
The childhood is learning to tell time. It is learning how hands move around and imagery is cyclical. But spirals down.

Clarification
When Georg was 4, Greta was 0. When Georg was 10, Greta was 5 or 6. When Georg was 15, she was 10 or 11. When 22, 17 or 18. When 27, 22 or 23. When 0, 23 or 24. When 0, 25, then 26. When 0, 0.

*

Now My Now
Today I was going to be flat like my brother Gregor, trapped in the room, revolting.
The mother's face a bruise, father qua brotherly invalid, voluble Victor dreaming up a future as a hotelier.
But the budding willow stole me! Pale green tongues hanging out of childhood with Hispanic seeds. Therefore hopeful Novalis. Things got new like girlish breast buds. Or she thrust her dainty nipples out.

To avoid being heckled.
Glorious, glorious! Conor's beard is trimmed, Reuben's stays thicker.
My crush on Reuben gets thinner as his beard gets thicker. It's ok,
there's another boy to love. Half-awake thoughts of the blond, his
hedge, his hard prick. Boy on tomboy swordplay. The universal was
blond. The guy coughed for Great Expectations, and I felt them! If
the reality principle's thin, choose transreality, not irreality?
Aria of sky and youth birch trees. Or honeysuckle bushes, white and
yellow. What is nature doing in this novel? Nature is the hovering
city.
A novelette because the good is in a hurry. Instantaneous perfection
momentary.
When his sister fell ill. Physics sang of string theory. Anton Webern's
collected works for string. Greta Trakl's recollected works for high/
strung out. She prefers the keyboard. Which is strings also, only
hidden. The universal vibration. Oscillation ontology! Some lady
said *vie-brato*.
But the word *this* is exploding! Uppers, because melancholy wasn't
pretty like Nick Drake. It was gruesome, horrid. Like Nick Drake. In
high school I played air guitar, my best friend Leila watched. God
played me, his instrument. Underlined the good with a pen. I got a
discount because of his marginalia. Juvenilia of my case.
As if my papa finally saved me. Or the world. With all its
possibilities. Rebel rebel in the head. The Smiths in the ears. But *now
I didn't wish I was not here.* Today not silent and gray. Rather, yellow
and orchestral.

*

Pearl Gray Notebook (Albeit Cross-Dressed)
Started high up. Clouds give off sparks! It's dangerous, still you do
it. My brothers almost make me forget my own philosophy. Georg,
Gregor, Ludvik, Victor, Haakon. Or the world climbs into my tower,
distracts my hair. From SK, paradox, irrationality, subjectivity.
From LW, showing not saying: subjectivity as unsayable. From
BS, aspectualism of modes, sense vs. reference, monism. From
FN, artistic metaphysics, *Über*something, will, return. From IK,
transcendental idealism, though individualized—so rebellious!
From AS, the world as will and presentation. But how to shed the
curse of narrative? Skip *Outcast Notebook* or *Cretan Notebook* for *Pearl*

Gray Notebook! What is incest semantics? What, incest metaphysics? Incest poetics! Thoughts flap around. The truth flower has three petals. The will to truth is the will to veracity, reality, fidelity. Via self-expression. It is a will to expression? With escape of self? Except this isn't thriving, since the light's too bright. It tore the cloud cover. If a girl woke up your hair, why won't she play with it? You have to play with it yourself, when writing. Otherwise the thoughts go flat.

*

LIGHT GRAY SLIGHTLY BLUISH NOTEBOOK
Agonistic foliage. There are no gray flowers. Awareness of mortality.

Because I am either hot or cold!

Work diligently or practice the piano with the black and white keys. To keep suppurating or supplicating. Greta 18 when moved to Berlin, still a minor key or poet? Fell for the landlady's nephew, Ferdl Thurstan.

Live the view, don't just propose it!

Everything looks better in this notebook, because my handwriting is better than it was before. Taller, more fervent. Hers was looping, like a clef.

Temperature, mercury, temperamental, mercurial! My brother Georg loved Saturn with its rings like haloes. I, Greta, loved Mercury with its silver-white like pearl gray.

Theses or phrases, teases or phases, musical pieces. Pitch, string. Maze. Maid. Coiled tune.

Matter is language? Content is meaning.

Musical language.
Function vs. motion.

Energy, expression, sound. Life!

Life or energy?

Desire for nothing vs. no desire. Desire for everything vs. some desire.

Yea and nay!

*

CHORD CHANGES
Desire doesn't stay still; death kills it, life revives it! Transience of truth, meaning, world. Why no structure. Only forces, motions, changes. No logos, word. Only sonos, sound. At the start was the sound, and the sound was of God, and the sound was God. The sound is life. But the words get in the way; they lie on the sound like a bullying brother. But couldn't they run together, become sound themselves?

*

HIGH RISK
Try it although you don't know how. Proclaimed herself a slut back when she was girlish Greta. The next morning, hot shame at confessional making a move or out or up. Sin to veer too close. Think the James Ensor painting: Christ entering Brussels. At least the bearded men w/ glasses have no appeal of ruling or verdict. And everywhere it's psychedelic rock like God. Yet maybe because of missing the silence, also misses the sounds. Should stroke the tongue. But distracted by details about that priest pulling down the pants of boys. What sort of adjective? You have all the evils in you. Last night's dream of working as a prostitute, then had to talk her way out of it. The older man, tall, slouched, bald w/ glasses, huge hands, baggy overcoat, wool cap. Asexual tenderness for the still-dark hair on his wrists. Now go away from the factual. It was pain, and she ran from it. Or the round-eyed cop raising the blue question of criminality. Yesterday's Feodor. Spurn him, still it isn't sounding right. So Greta, a cliff dweller in Wilmersdorf, reads cliff notes on Trakl. And it hurt, that I longed to put a father in this poem room. Could also be a sin tone. Anyway, there exists Georg, he could sub. Ditto Gregor. But insufficient. Feeling of inadequacy can lead to poetic violence or prosaic valiance. And no sound and no sound.

Plus I don't remember what page I was one. I meant on. Past a curse word in a different language. Something dishonest in this make-out session. Thus search for good influences. The forest hid. Lack of drama doused the stairs or Sabbath candles. Yesterday's fluorescence and madly shaking legs. An epileptic fit. Minus Feodor's ecstatic metaphysic. How come everybody's features look too big? They're coarse like Georg's and Grete's. Then a loud little old lady came to test our love. But Gregoire failed. Please axe this section. Head split by innocence. Red world spilling out.

*

FAINTLY BLUE SOMEWHAT PALE GRAY NOTEBOOK (DIVERTED)
Desire, striving, will. Oscillation is always active, but the will isn't?

Verse and reverse.

Low pitch vs. high pitch. Fever pitch! Her best pitch a curveball. Veering of effects, affects. Or a fastball. Fast vs. fast vs. fast. Like a girl who wants to be skinny, have no tits or hips.

Thinking subject vs. willing subject: two types of subjectivity. But subjectivity vs. the first person singular? And the object as the I? What is not the I, or doesn't have an I-coordinate? Nothing. But what is not *in* the I—

Is the oscillation the trajection?

Church bell. White truck.

Veridical subject vs. thinking subject vs. self-consciousness.

I as object, too? *I have black hair.* Actually it's turning bright gray: silver! Because I am so precocious. Being only 18. I mean 28.

The Silver Surfer was a comic book my brother Victor brought me.

Thought they were slaying the tree, but they were only pruning it. I fell into despair, then I leapt up and out of it.

My brothers were often very out of it.

The leaves start out green, then go yellow, then foliage brown in the fall.

The world is all that the fall is.

The ghosts of old sentences come back, hover.

I saw Stig the beautiful coffee jerker, he was tall with his medium gray wool hat, I wanted to take it off, play with his greasy hair. His right wrist had a fabric cast on it because he sprained it and played too much guitar. Now he has to use his left hand, the fingering, just the attack. Guitar solo for one hand. Should he be my new little brother or my younger boyfriend? Like Grete with Erhard, or Greta with Wladek. He said the guitarist with the song that's Kant's tower. Each philosopher has his own tower, it is his wilderness, desert, treehouse. Could the treehouse survive without the tree? Please do not cut down the tree! I saw the leaves vibrating, trembling, I saw the branches swaying. Some amputated limbs as with my brother Georg at the Galician front. We ate half a croissant, listened to neutral i.e. gray milk tones. But that's a different gray, not the unstable mix of black and white. Also, the tones weren't neutral, they cried out with passion while the boy sang as Stig would. Stig is wholesome and sweet, I said, Drink me like whole milk in elementary school with your sister, not like a mama! But he didn't hear me. I would lick the milk mustache off of him. His eyes are hazel, greenish.

*

ILL-EQUIPPED
So do it by homophones: through vs. through vs. through.
Or incompleteness as completeness: Gretel's paradox.
Students take incompletes
                         or pills with double meanings.
The treble muffled by the ringing in her ears from too much I love rock 'n' roll
and how nobody's interested in her boys' toys.
Her toying with ideas of others.
If I make it night now, will there be a deep and holy ring tone?

The metallic sanatorium so heavy to lift onto this desk.
It's said to be portable, but her back hurts from too many books. Like some scrawny Jewish precursor's heavy book baggage.
If she is reading, then Victor won't come near her is a fairy tale. Of sticky hands.
It could mean you lose your signage.
Age-inappropriate alarm clock. Appropriation of grown-up.
Crows. Or forlorn ravens. Transravens.
The people have lips.
I could say anything, that's what is
                                                    scary.
Some clumsy clapping, then Christ reentering Gotham from New Jersey.
Everybody laughed at Gregoire, who had to run away to a picture, which was not
any proposition but its negation.
The world is the totality of factures.
The collection of fractures.
I think I or she wrote that in some other abandoned book/notebook.
Oh my God, oh my God, why have
                                                    I forsaken you?
Vide Ferdek.
The set of all forsakings.
Why didn't they reproduce that one in valor?
James Ensor was a coloratura, while Gregoire is an antiheldentenor.
Her mouth should put on a shirt.
I don't deserve my freedom if I won't die for his
                                                    'n' her sins.

                                    *

GRAY BLUISH NOTEBOOK
Oscillation of the trajection as its movement, change. The knowing traject?

The *person* is thinking. The hunger, bad mood, greasy hair are thinking!

I = consciousness, self-consciousness, unconsciousness.

Make the unconscious yours, like your character per Ardl: unchosen but owned.

Subjective: related to I/subject. Objective: related to world/object.

Veridical subject: averring, thinking, feeling, fantasizing, perceiving, knowing, moving, thrusting, etc. subject. The I as motion, vibration: activity, not entity.

It's growing so hot here. Should I keep heading in this direction? Sometimes I want to rip my crotch off! If mentally frustrated, then sexually frustrated. Thought is lust.

Mind/body, subject/object: these distinctions not the same!

Lived body. Inhabited body, animated body? Don't know how to say it. Electricity connects the nerve words! Lived body an idiolect. I mean I am. But willful. So the body is lived from inside as will, not as known object. Then isn't there a willing subject? Why should the lived body be the immediate object—vs. an aspect of subject?

Or there is no subject/object distinction in my will, just fusion into singularity.

The solution to the mind-body problem: the mental state *is* the body mental, but undergone, possessed, directly experienced. Not observed, measured from outside. First vs. third person!

And if so-called externalism about the mental holds, such that different environments lead to different mental states (about my brother's metal shoulders; about the water he walked into), then it is the bodily state in that environment, but the body there as animated, and environment as encountered—

Greta, don't wander back into the academy! Grete likewise dropped out!

If the soul were another substance, it would be energy! But energy is of the body and vice versa. With no soul, the body is a corpse, a different *thing*. However, soul is not mind. Furthermore, what is spirit?

These terms hurt my wrist, it pulses nervously. Delicate faggy wrists that a bullying brother could snap by accident when he is trying to stop you from leaving, or holding you down. Or purposely hurting you in a sudden uncontrollable rage. But is that not pardonable?

The brothers resent their bodies or impose their bodies on you or both. You think, There must be another way to be in a body, to be as a body!

So the I is more than consciousness, self-consciousness, unconsciousness. It is also body. Or consciousness just *is* animated body?

Then what happens to me when I sleep and don't dream or if I faint: does the I cease to exist? Or is the I the whole nervous system, and consciousness just one aspect of that?

My brother Ludvik says, That is just the empirical I. But I say, It's also transcendental, there is no other. It's my transcendental wrist that hurts! From my repeated gestures, writing, thinking, it cries stop! From my being such a cleverpuss. But I can't stop because I am addicted! The concepts thrust themselves into me, I rub on them. Or I get overstimulated by teachers/crushes such as Ferdl and Ardl, the brothers charismatic! Although only in their writings. And finally they are contrary, so the younger brother Ferdl has to free himself from the older brother Ardl, ditto Greta from both of them. Like Eros vs. Thanatos. Or how Georg longed to die, while I, Greta, want to live! Don't I? But some questions are nonsensical. While others make sense. Like why should the living body ever be an object, be objectified? For sex is something else, sex object an oxymoron, sex subject the truth! But no, that's naive. Sometimes a person gets treated like an object. Especially a girl.

Ach, focus, Greta!

Object: what presents itself to me, to consciousness, to mind?

Pain as object? Feelings as objects?

I as consciousness swing, ride the swing: oscillate.

Recognizing oscillation as yourself: embodied creature as you, world as you, but not as subject.

No! Back out of that sentence.

Subject as not but, you as world, you as creature embodied: yourself as oscillation recognizing.

.tcejbus sa ton tub, uoy sa dlrow, uoy sa erutaerc deidobme: flesruoy sa noitallicso gnizingoceR

No! Back out of that strategy.

A willing I but not a subject? Is the I the subject, or does it go beyond it?

The *I think* vs. the *I am*.

He sips from a tiny straw, makes a sucking sound. Annoying!

The whole vampire motif. *Twilight* could also be an opera!

My betrothed Ferdl Thurstan was enamored of Reinhard Walter as of Ardl Sebastian with some homoeroticism, and Reinhard was of Ardl, so Reinhard Walter could write the opera, and it could be philosophical like Ardl. But *I* shall write the opera of Greta and Georg, and it will have a different philosophy!

Tempted by the libretto, wanders off, this is impasse.

*

GRETA & GEORG, OR SISTER AND BROTHER, OR TWILIGHT OF THE KIDS (THE LIBRETTO)

ACTING OUT I

Sehne 1

(Greta Tristl's bedroom in family castle/apartment. Greta, her aunt Marlene in locked room, Georg outside door.)

SONG OF CARPENTERS
(through window)
We've only just begun
To live
White lace and promises

GRETA
Whose LP taunts me?

(She strides to window at stage right, looks out. Across the way, two floors down, a young man in briefs does sit-ups; the music blares from his open window. Greta watches him for a moment, then turns around.)

Where am I?

MARLENE
You're in your room.
We're on your blue rug.
It's calm.
By evening, you'll feel better—

GRETA
Bitter.

MARLENE
Don't speak that way.

GRETA
(leans out of window)
Don't speak.
Unspeakable x.

MARLENE
(rushing to her, pulling her in)
What?

GRETA
Degenerate line! Unisex haircut.
Geschlecht ist schlecht.
It eats it.
Storm and sis. Suicidal blood.
Wet dream's self-spilled waking.
Shame's each.
He or I said, Let's split.
But together.
Now cowardly not to go alone.

MARLENE
What? I don't get it, but I fear it.
Or I fear getting it. Like leprosy.
Then God falls off your face.
But a unicursal maze is for simple tones.
The Master's plan.

GRETA
Enough!
Why can't you be Maria from *The Sound of Music*?
We had dream-sex once.

GEORG
(from other side of door)
Greta, I hear your slim figure!
Let me in!
Stony mother, drowning father.
Save my hair.

GRETA
(jumps back from door; to herself)
Stoned mother. Swallowed father.
Plunging brother. Falling sister.
Synopsis: sin op.cit.

Is it alright to stop early, after
Premature ejaculation?

Sehne 2
(Same place, 26 or 27 seconds later.)

SONG OF CARPENTERS
(through window)
I'm on the
Top of the world

GRETA
Light gray tones don't help.
Tight pink t-shirt.
They took away her street; its twin—
No, double—mattress.
Where's the stranger/youth?
Sleeps under the cover of *The Bedbugs Karamazov.*

MARLENE
Whom do you mean?

GRETA
Brother turns his eyes to mine.
We're shameful w/ hard nipples.
Eyebrow malfunctions. Or brows' dysfunctions.
Or being a function of two
Variables: love and despair.
Raise one abjection.

MARLENE
Tender youth, heldentenor.
You should let your brother in.

GRETA
Georg's a countertenor, you don't know him.
Would bite my neck,
Drink my voice. I need armor.

MARLENE
He needs comfort.
Let me let him in.

GRETA
I'm a contralto, you don't know me.
Would bite his back,
Stroke his eyes. I need fervor.

(Wladek arrives by Georg, grabs his arm.)

WLADEK
Still waiting for Greta? You should leave her, chill with Haakon! You
know she's betrothed to Ferdek.

MARLENE
(through door)
Georg, listen to Wladek.

GEORG
I listen for Greta.

MARLENE
She won't see you.

GEORG
Sister equals Holy Spirit,
I equal Son/Incarnation.
I went to Trinity High School,
She to Cathedral—no, Columbia.
Columbia means dove, *Trinity* means godhead.
Pale gray throat. Not slit. Metal shoulder blade.

MARLENE
Christ is like bedbugs: unstoppable.

GEORG
High school dances. I didn't dance.
The eyes leak chocolate milk. Gymnasium.

She spun Blondie, I played the Bee Gees.
She made brilliant music. Taught me taste.

MARLENE
You should stop recollecting.

GEORG
Abandoned garden.
Masculine despair:
Leafless. Leaden.
Cloud cover so the machine can
Be pushed around w/o
Pricking your sister's arm w/ your
Maroon thorn. Its. Organ shape.

MARLENE
You confuse yourself.

GEORG
Ourself. One sex. Two-headed boy.
Share the buried comic book.
Green flecks of decomposition.
Batman and Robin.
Green Hornet and Kato.
Kato a girl in one version.
Otherwise a Chinese man.

MARLENE
I liked their outfits.

GEORG
We wear our secret games, sleeveless.
On our wrists. The single gets scratched,
Is unprotected. Sex. Dead father snapped
Into the middle of our hole.
He was yellow.

MARLENE
Seek new music.

WLADEK
Like Greta does. Fickle bitch!
Learn to skateboard
Grow a 'stache, buy new kicks.
C'mon, bro; let's forget her.

Sehne 3
(Same old, same old.)

SONG OF CARPENTERS
(through window)
Hanging around
Nothing to do but frown
Rainy days and Mondays always get me down

MARLENE
(to Greta)
He won't go.

GRETA
What did he say?

MARLENE
Two-headed boy. Share the buried comic book—

GRETA
Decayed, dilapidated, expired, forfeited,
Addicted cemetery.
It's true that it was raining, therefore it is raining.
But I don't believe it. We dream.

MARLENE
Wladek mocked you.

GRETA
Once I marked him. My brother Haakon set us up.
But Wlad was too impressed with me. My music.

MARLENE
Georg called you a brilliant musician.

GRETA
Sometimes he's struck dumb.
I flow with notes.
Young man slender on sofa.
Wounded brow: Cain, Abel?
Tristl, diminished triad.
She saw him as her poor brother.
Their third: father. Another brow stroked,
But he turned into a strange man.
Sorrow. My brother intruded.
Anger. Then he gazed at me,
The green longing stung.
Sisterly, I consoled him,
We grieved. Until it pricked
Him, he ran out. Stupid story.

I said, Father!
Blue rain, graveyard.
Thought, Go to Ferdek, tutor.
But Georg returned
With pain milk.
Let's play 7 Minutes in Heaven.
Show me. I don't
Think we should do this.

MARLENE
I don't think I should hear this.
Familiar LP.

GRETA
What do you know of it?
No one knows.
Shame's yellow silence.
Tristl and Gretal went into the forest.
Mother as stepmother. Sorts her fine objects collection.
Father absent. He did not turn into an old man.

Dark. Cold. They need to stay warm:
Sister and brother. Silent.
Voluptuousness of death.
But betrayed the father. Cursed us.

MARLENE
Sorrow has confused you. Nothing happened!
Look how Georg wants you to go to Ferdek, develop.

GRETA
No he doesn't.

MARLENE
You need to have faith.

GRETA
I need to be unfaithful. Otherwise our father's curse—

MARLENE
(sotto voce)
Our father's.

GRETA
—makes this a death draft.

Sehne 4
(Boring dialogue working out logistics of Greta's planned escape: letting
Georg in, running out, locking him in.)

MARLENE
Georg! Wladek! Greta wishes to see her brother.

GEORG
Beloved sister!

WLADEK
Aagh! Screw this!

(He runs away; Marlene opens the door. Georg rushes in and up to Greta.

They stare intently at each other. Greta struggles to compose herself.)

Sehne 5
(After rapid breathing.)

GEORG
Darling! Greta!

GRETA
Did you think my plan would change? Don't you know that I must leave you?

GEORG
You can't leave me.

GRETA
Marlene, leave us.

(Marlene nods conspiratorially, exits, waits outside.)

GRETA
Your lamed smile clouds my resolve,
Resounds in abandoned room.
Sister, dark asylum,
Brother, decayed signage, longer eyes
Press question mark, other key or star
Your machinery eludes me.

GEORG
Night room w/ glowing plastic stick-on stars
Damnation's strange decor
But your room flowers
Silent petals, single word stem. Stalk.

GRETA
Petals flutter, eyelids seeking
Blindness, not flirtations. Father's voice
Belonging to a dead man.

Who called for grayness. Horror.

GEORG
The brother shall not look there.

GRETA
From fear of what?

GEORG
Ask our babysitter.

GRETA
She left us alone. Anyway, you dissemble.

GEORG
Disassembled. Desolate wood
Floor of childhood lore
Undiscerning. Sister! Hasten closer.

GRETA
Blutschuld swings between us. Do you remember
The swing on the weeping willow tree?

GEORG
Blue shoulders. Blue touch, hold.
Language a foreign element. Atonal.

GRETA
Chords progress with tender fingerings.
Shiny. Yellow.

GEORG
Do not say it, show it only.
Play it slowly.

GRETA
Shadow's stammering semantics.
But no back pedal.
Shaved heads. Sustain petal won't atone.

GEORG
Sonata for masculine despair. In G-minor.

GRETA
Pale brother fading in his cords,
Buried in his purple hair.
Or blue and black, *übermenschlich*.

GEORG
That would be you. A youth in metal.
Silver breastplate, fauld, greaves. *Jüngling*.

GRETA
Tinfoil and cardboard sword fights.
Secret games in the dusk square park.

GEORG
Furtive playtime. Dirt-stained knees.

GRETA
Brooding brother's hand-off. I stayed
Mine there. Betrayed a deductive vow.

GEORG
What vow?

GRETA
Reaching for my dad.

GRETA AS GREGOIRE
Green or gray or blue? Not sure if this works here. Trapped
libretto. They pulled up, stalled. She walked past the foreign one,
bared her legs. Smooth young skin on the back of his neck. No new
symbol. Polish double-parking. Sick and weak syntax. Grieved,
aggrieved semantics. Where is bold Isolde? Extremist shapewear.
Twilight's undergarments.

GEORG
If you were or would be his,

Then you score me. Snap me in two.

GRETA
I'm going to Ferdek!
I won't scar you.
Please don't scare me, brother.
I need to improve my
Improvisations. Also, he needs me—

GEORG
I need you.

GRETA
I am your illness.

GEORG
My wholeness. Holiness.

GRETA
Don't be ridiculous. Unholy idiot.

SONG OF CARPENTERS
(*through window*)
We can't stop
Hurting each other

GEORG
Where are we?

GRETA
In a bad act. With too much sense.

GEORG
Sensuality. Let's be silent.

GRETA
(*moving to door*)
That's escapist. Listen,
I need to change my address
From *Greta bei Weltschmerz, Tod, Georg*

Or Greta@sorrow.Georg.
Be a stranger like our father. Father—

GEORG
(grabs her, pulls her to window)
Two-tone apostrophe. Why do you address
Him? Undress me, dress my wound.
Bad skin's confession. Leprous adolescent.
Don't leave me! You can't leave me. Let us
End it here, w/ a death duet. Carpenters = *Zimmermänner*
= young men of the room, but we flee it—

GRETA
Georg!

GEORG
Greta!

GRETA
Fearless brother.

GEORG
Free-verse sister.

(They stand clutching each other before the window.)

SONG OF CARPENTERS
(through window)
I won't last a day
Without you

MARLENE
(bursts into room)
What are you doing?
Oh, not that, but this
Is worse! Children, stop it!

GRETA
Get out! Leave us alone!

MARLENE
But—

GRETA
Leave now, or Georg will make you leave. He has dissociative rages.

(At her words, he advances toward Marlene.)

MARLENE
(backing out)
Just like Antoine.

GRETA
How could I leave you?

GEORG
How could I let you?

GRETA
Guilt's brilliant belt.

GEORG
Shame's glinting shirt.

GRETA
Desperate reading.

GEORG
Violet wrestling.

GRETA
My Tristan!

GEORG
My Iseult!

GRETA
Savage boy.

GEORG
Scorching girl.

GRETA & GEORG
In the chest lay the hands
As black birds, or ink black night's
Beautiful spill, or black and
Blue bruises or superheroes' hair
With arias for highlights.
These voices the same,
Dawn star = dusk star,
Hit twilight notes.
Then bared backs
Or violence of blunt guilt.
Whose meaning's secret.
Nothing else matters but this
Instant—

(They embrace, kiss, go further. Marlene opens the door, watches. The ghostly figure of Antoine comes up behind her to look. Greta catches sight of them over Georg's shoulder, freezes, pushes Georg away. He laughs as if she's teasing him, reaches for her, but she backs off, shakes her head. He frowns, grabs her hard. She shoves him back. He slaps her so she stumbles. He tries to take advantage, but she kicks him. They wrestle. She bites him. He throws her to the ground, kicks her. A frozen moment. Then he stares down at her, horrified. She springs up, rushes past him, locks the door behind her, keeps running. Dead Antoine has vanished. Marlene stays by the door. Georg runs to it, bangs on it.)

GEORG
Greta! Sister! I'm sorry! Greta, come back!

SONG OF CARPENTERS
(through window)
I'll say goodbye to love

*

SOUNDCHECK
Inconsequence clicks or
            plinks of heat
                  with voices wafting.
Arm-waving diversionary tactile learning fingertips
                  sawed-off shot pen.
Leave room for the windows. They should be big windows, not
bricked up, broken, impoverished.
                  Or motion as of planets, comets,
                  like Jupiter with all the moons
in that girl's mouth
                  because the girl, the sister
                              did not
                              know them.
            It doesn't matter.
But sirens say jump.
Or rope or
            crash your
                  machine or lap
                  event of action
                  truth as interpretation
                  thought if thing
                  word unless object
                  mind but world
                  crime with punishment
                              was that
                              bad?
The surging sounds as of cool metallic generation
                              like of
                              battles.
Lost limbs of arguments.
But swallowing everything as you
                  then expelling it
                        shit or full of
                        it or trashy
like that woman's splotchy tights.
The sounds should save you
                  but they don't always save you,
nor his sonata-

problem with the private-form
sonata-form of private sentence.
But scared to write a symphony
                    or symphonic poem though in prose.
Or tone poem or a poem tone
was getting away from her
bird circulars
groaning stalling
                    or replenish
                              lightbulbs looked up.
Or abstract sounds
                              dragging the poetic feet
          no conversational German
                              impure dial tones
breaking rules
          as if to answer
                    is she still living?

TWILIGHTS
In the first one she was kind of interesting, edgy, smart, funny; in
the second she was just pathetic, dependent, a drag. Insecurity,
self-hatred. Like Greta with Bibi. Then Leila's like Alice. At least
Bella was risky for a reason other than self-destruction. I think she
could've been cool if the movie had been written, directed, acted
differently. The basic premise of seeking danger just to see him is
somewhat hot. I will convert you, said the one girl to the other girl.
But Leila said no. Back then, Greta didn't yet have fangs, while Bibi
still had eyebrows. Both girls skinny, sad. The boys more like Jacob,
compact, kind of animal, wiry, big lips, small eyes. Dub one Cal, the
other Max. Bella acts like Cal aka James Dean in *East of Eden*, actually.
Or James Dean's character in *Rebel Without a Cause*, I can't recall his
name now. Oh yeah, it's Jim. Bibi and Greta were in love with James
Dean. Then Greta bought a red zippy jacket to be him. Only she was
too expressive, verbal. Vs. coiled, internal, physical frustration and
constraint. This language too damn conversational! I was supposed
to be doing research on Austrian and German Expressionist writers
or writing sound-based poetry. *Re Bella: Without a Cause.* She needs
some kind of talent, passion other than Edward's wavy dark hair
and sparkly gold skin. How come he doesn't start burning like

Spike in *Buffy*? Sunlight should be dangerous. You could expose yourself by taking your shirt off, then they'd see you are a girl, the mob would kill you. Gold-leaf nipples. 'Cause sometimes she passed herself off as Gregory, a boy. Doing dumb things like climbing that monument drunk, or dashing across 86th Street high, or wandering through the park at night tripping w/ a guy you barely know. Vs. the other one. Will *he* come back to save her? You should stay away from me, I'm bad for you. He already had fangs. Those such as us prefer cloudy days, rain and melancholy. On the other hand, we can travel fast across mountains, in woods, be in a fantasy or fairy tale. I'm too old for you. But you look so young and boyish. Years later, *she* is too old for *him*. If purely in numbers. Greta always precocious, which finally doesn't make her old, it makes her frozen, stunted. I want you to have a normal life. But I don't want that, I would rather be dead with you. Alien. But now I feel tired and kind of stupid, weak; think I'll do more research on somebody who's other. The images of him as a phantom, floating before her and warning her, were idiotic-looking, kitschy. Forgot to see the street again. Female bum yelling at male bum. Vagrants fighting at the language-game tables. Stony Ludvig or Georg. I am their sister, sometimes feel the same nothing. Don't walk there or they'll call you faggot. I might watch the first movie once more, try to get inspired. I liked Jacob better with long hair, except when it looked fake. Greta liked boys with long hair, they were sexy if they had faces that were ok. The violet flowers are on spindly trees, not bushes, I double-checked.

*

GRETA & GEORG, ANTI-LIBRETTO (*MENSCH*, I DON'T KNOW HOW TO WRITE THIS WITHOUT SOUNDING KITSCH!)
ACTING OUT II
Sehne 1
(*Dark café in Berlin. Greta and Antoine stand amidst shabby furniture, he holds her arm to warn her against Georg—No, skip it, sub something else!*)

GRETA OR GREGOIRE
What's going on, bro? Not her aria, but a bus stop gesture. Banged my knee so hard into the metallic corner of my ambition, I almost went labyrinthine. The youngest profession? On the street, a tall black chick maybe with a dick says, Hello Handsome to Gregoire. Or

asks How you doin', Handsome? Logic of question vs. exclamation.
Nobody shot sentences. Palm readers absconded with our electricity.
Two forests on a pale man's shoulders. The sound yellow and gray.
Punishment of rereading. Or a young priest who refused to offer
me rest. The Flash dons his Robert Rauschenberg painting, zooms
off like Friedrich or Friedrich. Flashed some desire: priority male.
Parcel post for Gregoire's ghostly package. Phantom opus #*n*. At
some point, I will have to burn my fillings like Isolde. Last-minute
find and replace indicates Boethius' color wheel. But the picture
theory shows its limits, flaunts its plexi. Still it's perky: offers perks
of metaphysics. Nipples. Behind the shades were *Sturm* windows,
they were tired. In the head shop, buy an orange plastic concept
with a metal faith bowl: thumbnail grail or bauble. High school rap
sheet turns to sheet music. Water dies when iced. Greta freezes the
frame job. Back to black, shiny, a time when Gregoire still stuck on
the world, understudied something as novitiate. The mouth licks
mad lips. Dry mounting's learned pretty quickly. Vs. chamber music.
It's good for impoverished visuals such as opera posters. Now I will
be Greta, poster girl for pain via foam core. Or mouth foam, like
epileptic tune. The unplayed music? Wait—

*(Greta turns her head away from Antoine, hearing running steps. Georg
bursts into the café, halts. They stare at each other. Run forward, embrace
fervently.)*

GEORG
Greta, *Geliebte!*

GRETA
Georg, dear sibling!

GRETA & GEORG
Bruise of meaning habit's dark lure or unquelled lore uncanny
mirrors unisex breast o my brother/sister wake to licks of
psychedelic silver dis their eyes dismiss their minding hear din's
hurts because we like it the kindred drug dream soul of oneness
shining hearse or hearsay deadly lust without difference without
distance super-I's supersiblings or one I androgynous being Tristolde
undreamt illogical connective mine Tristan's mien of full meanings

mine Isolde's mien means of dying evict it evade it every isolation's mask Greta Georg ever after single Greorg no foreign longing so weird this nearness so near this weight and weightless feeling could not wait!

GEORG
Did you think you could lose me? He stood there before her, burning in his orange hair.

GRETA
I thought to leave you in the dark. The sister ran away to a starving older man.

GEORG & GRETA
Usw.

(Georg and Greta exit café, walk hand-in-hand through garden with flowers. Antoine's ghost steps from behind tree. The siblings halt.)

GRETA AS GREGOIRE
Wovon man nicht schreiben kann, darüber muss man schweigen. Make father do a dumb show signing no-no. Sibs ignore him, make out with loud sucking noises. Even bite. Then they turn into one prose poet with an androgynous voice that projects—

GREGOIRE AS GREGOIRE
Which, now, surprises the viewer aka listener. He said, Sorry, bro! Oh, I mean sorry, miss. Was a stranger. The noisy girl left with her orange self-Hi-Liter. Ferdl says, Come all over yourself. Hand-in-hand the siblings foam. Georg, Greta! The names have to be retired numbers. I hold him in me, he holds me in him: latent, blatant. That song finally shot itself. Not her brother Victor. Only Georg's night and its tight fit like the dark blue pants. Tall strangers in white shirts vanish. Also the man's yellow shoe she/I thought could save us if we carried it into a poem. Squeezed his pectoral strain, red and yellow couldn't hit the pitches. The open silver beckons weirdly. And the black and white horror blanket. Hunger plucks a violet thing. Shiny violet-black truth table with two values: tools and falsies. Then break up pragmatic theory. Such thoughts don't rest on Georg, they

peel off. The house of dying adults. Stony shag rugs. TV eroticism. *Dark Shadows.* Someone's working on this remotely. *If you leave, would you just tell me?* Left alone by the governess, who is made of spiritual plastic. Trading lost baby teeth, marbles, comic books or phobias. My hair on his head, his eyes in her mouth. Her nostrils in his eyebrows. Let's play handball. In the hall of infamy: this shadow's hallway, its Spaldeen. End of grief. But the theme stayed underdeveloped or overly varied. Still loyal under-one-another-studies. Trees shudder in the breeze of brother/sister weather system. Systematic failure. Georg's mouth slid off his weak cleft chin, his wet hands fluttered. Greta stumbled, hit her brow, developed a concussion, world. Georg wrenched his index finger. Why aren't they one crayon? Violet-blue not the same as blue-violet in the Crayola box. Still both wrote twilights. Permissive missives. Tender. It has nothing to do with mystical loss of self, oceanic feeling or renunciation. But the music: let it muss us. We were the hairs on father's head. Mass noun romantics. Rub this with an explosion or plosive of a handjob. Brother on the balls of the feet, sister on the heels: I remember. Holes hammered by others' horror. Secret double exposure of the negative equals positive of the dream. The night's more should not have said I—

WLADEK
(rushing in)
Save yourself, Tristls!

(Ferdinand/Ferdek/Ferdl in Superman t-shirt and Adelhard/Ardl in aristocratic finery enter the garden. Antoine backs out, disappears. Georg and Greta turn from each other to face Ferdek and Ardl but continue to hold hands. Street lamps go on.)

*

INTERLUDE / INTERMISS
Victor liked Superman, Greta loved Spider-Man, while on Gregoire's black t-shirt, Batman runs in profile in front of the tiny grand city. The Chinese mathematician scribbled numbers, peered through wire glasses, wore shorts. Showing how it was to believe you could be the greatest, have profound insights, as did Ferdek. Snowy mountains in his future like in my past's book. Wild Swiss mangod. Dark

socks to prevent developing a coward's cold feet. Female shame kept me from breathing properly. Nietzsche is a maroon voice, Greta is a sluttish bookmark. Young dark-haired vagrant crumpled up in a doorway, sleeping: a marionette. Question of the essence of the world: conatus/ceaseless striving will to survive vs. will to overcome (oneself, others if necessary), i.e. to power. Greta thinks a will to motion, change. Dynamics as of their duo. His power idea too progressive. Life is energy. Heraclitus' view closer to Greta's than Nietzsche's. But why let informal philosophy intrude on the libretto? Because the Chinese genius twirled the pen in his fingers, it helped him think math. Plus the opera *Tristan und Isolde* was *itself* philosophy, namely Ardl's. While that lady uttered expletives to herself. Fantastic t-shirt. Thanks! My rubber pale sanitorium green. I mean my rubber band. It's not a rubber room, so I haven't been locked up yet. Try to use your empathy to be Ferdek now. He fought against his. *I feel the pain of everyone, then I feel nothing.* His sweetly rough male voice. Sometimes I feel so much, sometimes I am so coldly unmoved.

*

PEARL I.E. SLIGHTLY BLUISH MEDIUM (OR LIGHT) GRAY NOTEBOOK
In the world or outside it.

To the side. Before they pick you for their team in swim class. I only wish to swim with Georg.

The philosophical ideal of indifference, invulnerability a syphilitic temptation. Why feel safe? Why want to?

The pearl removed from the shell. But its small hard lustrous body.

How the sister's body glows in the moonlight or starlight in his poetry.

If the world is pure suffering, then you want to leave it.

Or to stay, to love it?

While the other philosopher says vitality. I mean my betrothed,

Ferdl.

To stop time, lose your I, evade subject and object by silencing your will.

But the will is a *force*, not a subject. And desire, power and energy evade time in another way.

If all the moments already exist, are laid out like a music score, in a space, and you could move from one to another, out of sequence. Or read right to left. Or behold them all at once.

The view *sub specie aeternitatis*?

Then the sorrow of transience, loss, death ceases? But the truth *is* mortal—so the immortal moment's neither true nor false? Or it's another type of truth? And being mortal is exactly what lets you leap out of mortality—into the present moment, which could be a repeat of the past or a fantasy of another possible world.

The extremist solipsist says only this now with this I exists. But then what do *now* and *I* mean? Once there's nothing to contrast them with, they vanish. Solipsism becomes mysticism. But why must *that* be will-less?

If music directly expresses the will via temporality, it also bring the deepest experiences of eternity, transcendence. There's a connection.

The aim is not to cease wanting, it's to want more deeply—be pain and rapture's instrument!

Gray a disguise for black and white, suffering and ecstasy? So the gray notebook is a secret composition book.

Payne's—pain's!—gray, bright gray, stone gray are all the senses of my gray, the referent. It doesn't follow that they don't conflict.

Ferdl's critique of Ardl's negativity, passivity, asceticism: it's how I could become infatuated with Ferdl, think that he would save me.

But then he didn't save me. I was repulsed by his stiff, unnatural, forced sexuality. Not like my beautiful, languid brother's.

Is suffering the only truth, the way to truth? That's what Georg thought. And Feodor encouraged him.

But the truth and the way to truth are different, aren't they?

Or not.

I look at the ones who do not suffer or feel the suffering of others, they frighten and appall me.

My notebook is plain. It is naked. Is it too naked?

I don't know how to write my notebook, so I keep starting over.

But that is not eternity.

I cried out, Fragility! Vulnerability!

A pearl is hard and shiny, though it can be crushed or cracked or chipped. Then, supposedly, it's worth less. Not that I fondle jewelry; I am not my mother's daughter. I fondle myself, or let my brother Georg fondle me. My words, his words. How they touch each other.

I am my father's daughter. I am my brother's sister.

This was supposed to be about Ardl vs. Ferdl, then I got distracted by sex. They'll say, How like a girl!

*

GRETA AS GREGOIRE

Now *this* should be a full opera scene about Ferdl/Nietzsche, his philosophy when he meets Lou Salomé, and then when she deceives and dumps him for Paul Rée. The narrative of being betrayed by two friends/pupils. How Lou said, Let's love/live as brother and sister. How Paul fixed them up. Ferdl's lament, resentment, rage, *Unübermenschlichkeit*. Instead it's bad like Ferdl's/Friedrich's poetry, so make it a prosaic quickie:

GEORG & GRETA, THE *NOCH NICHT ÜBERLIBRETTO*
ACTING OUT II
Sehne 2
(Same garden, 2 nows later.)

ARDL
See, brother, I told you! Proof gives hope the finger. So you're saved
by the gall!

FERDEK
How am I saved, when this proof's a Gottblock? Crimps my self-
stylings, jams my sustain pedal.

GRETA
Daybreak's dealer of heroic dream idioms, touching, mad egoist! I
swing, I vanish.

FERDEK
So he'll be your mirror? Because of his sickly guilt and glam cosmic
bad boy's *Nein*? Why lip services of yore to my will, our zeal's
genius? Now I just seem a schmuck. Poor stupid hermit! I was
willing to put away my Übercrotch for you! I should've listened
to my sister Elzbieta's bile. And Georg, you introduced her to me,
wanted her to be my heir, escape the glum curse, Daddy issues. So I
accepted her self-denial thing; who could resist her bold machismo?
Not to mention her whip smarts and virtuosity. But what did you
two do? Aagh, she's childish, a fake female, a scrawny stinking *Affe*,
affect, ape—aping opera! And your deception exposed my baser
balls, my low leitmotives. This is the fiercest test of my affirmative,
self-overcoming metaphysics. Was my vision a phantom limn, not a
prophecy? Is there no gain from pain, worthwhile fight for *amor fati*?
(He starts doing push-ups like DeNiro in Taxi Driver. *Greta and Georg
stare.)*

GEORG
Mensch, cunning Ferdek, I don't know! Greta, are you coming with?
Georg will share his goth eyeliner with you.

GRETA
Yes! Our secret house whispers sweet nothing. Tugs at Greta's sleeve like a brother. But can we drop the third-person? My philosophy's against it.

(They suck face. Ardl starts forward, furious.)

ARDL
Harlot! Ha! The opposite of self-transcending! Sheer dirt, lust!

(Georg flushes, stares immobilized at Ardl. Greta turns to face Ardl.)

GRETA
Hater! Ah, the hypocrite of self-transcending. *(Georg flinches.)* Sheer spite, pride! You no longer tempt us to your weak, life-hating gloom, your high mystic passivity. With your envy, anger, you betray your own ideal of purity—

(Georg gasps, runs off. Greta, shocked, moves to follow. Ardl pushes her, she falls, hits her head, passes out. Wladek cradles her. Ferdl turns on Ardl with horror. Ardl bolts.)

*

SHOWING, NOT SAYING. AND DON'T CHAINSMOKE THEM!
How Reinhard's music is much better than his libretto! And Ferdek had to dump *him* in the end, too—after so much hero-worship. As Greta will have to dump all of them! Not her heroes: her hangers-on, with their hang-ups! Oh Bondage Up Yours! Can I abort this version?

*

HARD FACTOIDS
This isn't yours, right? A man's warm smile. Awake. Alarm cock. Her gorgeous clavicle. Or laughter like a rug. The green leaves glow prepubescently. Total unity of writer and writing. Perfectly shaped sideburns as pledges. Karl Unkraus's clear distinction between fact and value a prosthetic message. If each sentence shows the moral/aesthetic character of the writer, integrity or lack of it, then so does each asserted fact. The feminine/masculine opposition absurd, but

fantasy vs. reason? He sighed through his noseholes, leaned forward. Shrieking lacks grammar. They said Expressionist lyrics, I said music. The apple lit up with the first bite. Greta Trakl rubs her blurs. He restocked the straws so they could be grasped at. My body isn't liquid. Paper.

I FORGOT
I forgot about my brother Victor. He didn't call me. Is he sad now?

MOUTH MATH/SEX SETS
Intersection set of full lower lip w/ a stranger. Name him Omar. Omar, bang me!

AGAINST NIHILISM
Anything's ok. Anything's better than nothing. Says the breath test.

PROFANED CONSTELLATION
The things get layered, change scales. A fly graces the chair. Walter Benjamin enters in striped sweats. If it's too thick for you to lift, *a fortiori* to read, still you can point to it. Ripped sugar packet. Every phrase is perfect because it *is*: reality's perfection. The cold draft on my neck was two pages long w/ some cross-outs. It has to go now. Feodor's cracked knuckles. Plasticity of running notes. I.e. away.

*

BRIGHT GRAY SLIGHTLY BLUISH NOTEBOOK
Thicket of ideas about the subject. Different aspects vs. different subjects: it can't be reduced to an essence, e.g. expressing or averring. Also the standard subject/object distinction is leprous. And Ardl was wrong about a pure knowing subject—or, *that* subject is not the I!

Verifying subject: *I* am the proof!

Fear of losing yourself to your brothers! They want to invade you.

The storm fell silent, now a bright gray. A cool breeze. Forget about humiliations. No true intimacy with anyone. Misunderstood clouds.

Subjectivity as personal: the first person singular. So I and subject *are* the same— whereas consciousness is less?

It's *my* consciousness! The *structure* of truth universal, the relata not. But demoting consciousness. My brother Lukerl. My betrothed Ferdl.

A shirtless young man doing crunches across the way, two floors down.

The 10 year-old girl in the TV masturbated to the TV, got into trouble.

Some weird vibration in my head. Its light grayness.

To occupy a view, be the viewing I, is not simply ocular.

The relation between view and oscillation. The viewing subject *is* the vibrating subject!

Greta wrote ideas in a flash flood, scared off the others with her egoism. Only the egoism of boys is viewed as attractive.

The young man stands up, he's wearing white briefs, walks away across his floor.

The gray is growing too bright, I feel exposed like a bad inference.

The relation between truth and vibration: truth demands oscillation.

Thoughts lead you, there's no other guide such as a brother, father, mentor. The guide is your *secret* thinking subject. Because so much stays unconscious.

The avowing subject. The avouching subject. But space beyond veridical space—so truth's too narrow after all? Or what is the truth of fantasy?

The world is all this, which is fictive.

Will to power vs. will to truth—thus says Ferdl Thurstan. But, too, the will to powerlessness.

The young man returns naked, he's oblivious to Greta. Does she want to have his prick or hold it? Why not both: be a girl with a dick, as in those Henryk Danger paintings!

Actually, right now I just feel like having a slit.

The swinging single subject!

Car horn solo, not the horn in that symphony by Gustaff. Ferdl improvises on the piano; he sweats and forgets me. Even though *I* am supposed to be the keyboardist.

His will to power, eternal recurrence, perspectivism, *my* will to veering, eternal oscillation, first personalism.
I am unhappy with my betrothed. I wrote a prose poem to Georg.

If the I is an axis, how can it be a moving point? If a moving point, how an axis?

The I-axis is not the I, because the I-coordinate keeps shifting. The shifting subject. Metaphysical oscillation, veridical oscillation: the same?

Force of oscillation, eternal variation, first personalism! The truer triad, chord, trinity. Divinity is creativity, expression!

Oscillating between two points vs. veering between many? The swinging subject. The veering subject. Swing: 1) oscillate; 2) shift, change, turn. E.g. one's view, attention. So the oscillating underwrites the veering! But how is it related to truth?

The proof of this is *my* experience! Cyclothymia, bipolarity. Metaphysics of bi!

The sentence itself vibrates between expression of belief (subjective) and assertion of fact (objective).

The truth vibrato. The averring subject of the I *is* a vibrating subject or I.

Is the averring subject a subset of the swinging subject? Then my truth graph is a fragment. So it's wrong to reduce everything to truth.

Force of oscillation (intensity, energy), eternal veering, first personalism (including a will to truth). *Ja*, ok!

Can intensional space (vs. extensional Cartesian space) be graphed, scored, plotted?

Will to intensity or to lack of intensity. Sometimes you crave loss of power. Like all my brothers and I. The desire for the ghostly feeling. The dream, its unreality.

The young man shut off the light. Left his apartment? Greta decides that he is Omar.

The holy sister a ghost because her brother doesn't see her. Or, only he sees her.

My betrothed sees only himself, thinks Greta.

This level of abstraction is debilitating me, must I still sacrifice myself to it? To being the *explicit expression* of the first person singular. Not just its incarnation.

The task of the Holy Spirit/ Ghost. Unholy poet, guest. Adolescent, too much!

The Overmuch.

*

THE MUSIC YOU AREN'T HEARING
Sisterly languor. No, it was her brother Gregor who lay in bed, could not convince himself to rise. Maybe if you—don't say it. Tired of the various blues: dusk, midnight, electric, cerulean, ballpoint.

This requires more lube. Too hurried. But we thought you were fast. It's cold in the brow of the forest. A brother appears from a machine. Honeysuckle bushes: white and yellow. If you climb down, you won't be able to climb back up. Greta's cliff as clef. Branches waved goodbye to the day. Her chest curled protectively around her chest organ. She bit her mouth organ. He licked an Edvard Munch painting named *Melancholy*. *His book's in the library. I don't know if people use the library.* Austrian vs. Swiss accent. Chewed the pencil while being chewed out by the first principle, our principal? My brother had fluffy hair, my other brother had wavy hair, my other brother had long straight hair, my other brother had close-cropped wooly hair, my other brother had combed-back wiry hair.

*

CRUSHED FLOWER
Fell in love with another skinny boy flower w/ black petals of t-shirt and loose jeans cuffed high, black socks on slim ankles, narrow black deck sneakers. He has short fluffy dark hair, a thin mustache, a rash of pimples on one side of his face, a deep voice, small wiry body, thin arms, high hairline on back of neck, dark thin slanted-up hazel eyes, oval face, beautiful cheekbones, put too much milk in my coffee, it's cold now, I think his name should be Jesse. Can't concentrate in here.

DECISION
Actually it turned out that he was my brother Victor, who sometimes could be younger. A naif.

PRECISION
Then I realized who Victor was! How he changed his name to Vincenzius to be a frou-frou Romantic.

GRETE TRAKL, GRETA TRAKL
Found the keyboard in the gutter of the page. Grete a gifted pianist, four-and-a-half years younger. At 26, shot herself in the adjoining room of the book of poetry. Used his 7, only had a 6, she/her world truly and perfectly unfinished. An abortion complicated matters like all of those uncompleted novels. She took his 7 because of the acute angle. Or you reach the apex, then backTrakl to the starting point but on a higher level. Or as if leaping, offing faith. And the shape

of a gun that is gunmetal gray. Suicide a tautology. The publishing party? *Der Sturm*: Expressionist exclamation points and periods. Dusk threatening the forehead. Weaponized thoughts. Georg overstimulated is one option. But see the three junior high boys, Arab or Latino, w/ their skateboards. Observations oppressing the imaginations like brother does sister. I don't know how to find out more about Grete. *It's better to kill yourself to pass the exam.* Together in Vienna. Later she was in Berlin, he was in Vienna or Salzburg or Innsbruck. Their intersex briefs lost or destroyed. The girl aggressive, the boy passive is the convention. The mother Maria abstracted, obsessed with her hoarded ancient worry beads. Perhaps a secret sorrow. Don't put too much in here, save it for later. But Grete always rushed things. Refracted or distracted handwriting. Using stimulants. Meanwhile not returning Victor's calls, or Grete didn't visit Berlin as escape. She married, he didn't. Brother and sister can't get married. The interest in older men such as Markus, Warren, that camp counselor Lee. Nostalgia as drug. Or amnesia. The girl an addict. Stop this, it's like making out with someone you aren't really attracted to. It has bad breath and opens its mouth too wide and wet. It has no loveliness.

PICTURE OF EXTREMIST AS A YOUNG MAN/GIRL
Young Ludwig, young Georg: obsessed with rigor, crystalline purity. Whereas Greta goes for loose mixtapes, mixtypes.

*

LUKERL & GRETEL
The fairy tale. Holding hands in the forest. Not ready to decipher the dusk progression. Crumbs eaten by students who talk too much. Aphorisms' ephemera. Not ready to walk though the story.

GRETE MEANS SISTER
Ludwig had a sister named Grete, she was his favorite. Sophisticated, intellectual, older-seeming, I mean precocious.

PEARL OF GRETA'S PRICE
The brother would trade everything for the sister. No, that was Georg.

CONTRAST

He unlocked his machine, she did not have a machine. Yet constantly
switched gears. Can a machine think? *Kann ein Mädchen denken?*

BROTHER & SISTER

The brother's big face. Petals larger. Trees in courtyard with birds.
What I want to show you. Brother and sister play show and don't
tell. Her flaw ineliminable. Black ink stain of resentment spreading
over the white sheet. The pen is mine. Don't you see the decay?
He doesn't see it. I don't know how to write it. Walked together.
The unconditional a fantasy. The unconditioned. Romanticism's
fragments. A metaphysical arrow, as of Ishmael. I know what this
should be about, therefore I can't write it. *In my own estranged way,
I've always been true to you.* Night complaint. Then he climbed to
the cloud chamber, she descended to the cellar. Light stripes the
buildings sideways. Conor wears a wide-striped sweater: red, blue,
gray. Marcus the younger plays *Now people are good, and people are bad,
and I'm never sure which one I am.* Silver Jews like silver unborn ones
in Trakl. Theme of exile. The lanky sailor Billy says, Conor, look how
cute you look today. And he does. Today is beautiful. I could love my
lovely big brother without reservation, I could cancel my reservation,
I could not show up at the resentment restaurant, I could be a good
little sister and get collagen on my chest pump, which pumps love.
The oil spill in the ocean uncontainable, it's killing all the birds in
my brother's courtyard. But we could be different. The guilt flaps
up and away, and joy's a door with a shift lock. Victor remembered
huge circles of bright colors, plastic or Colorforms, not chloroform.
I couldn't remember them. Oh my brother. Then they went into
the forest to look at honeysuckle bushes. Gentle playmates in the
evening. My brother's eyes are innocent even though they're not
round.

*

DARKLING BUT STILL LIGHT GRAY BLUISH NOTEBOOK

A notebook is a labyrinth.

Labyrinthitis an inflammation of the inner ear aka labyrinth, leading
to dizziness, nausea, visual disturbances such as a naked young man

or a father with a penknife or upside-down trees in Central Park from some hallucinogen.

They hypnotize the hysterics to try to cure them of their labyrinthitis. Are they considered conscious, semi-conscious, unconscious? In a sleeplike state?

Lately, bad sleep. Nightmares, insomnia. Can you say *I* in your sleep and mean it?

Self-consciousness not the aim, highest function. Gregor, Ludvig, Georg feared it!

Loss of sense of self while creating. But no view without consciousness. The subject *is* conscious but is more than consciousness. *A fortiori* more than self-consciousness.

It thinks in me (Ferdl!) vs. I think.

What does *I* refer to and mean? Oh, what is it? *The I, the I is what is deeply mysterious!* So scrawled my brother Ludvig.

The I transposes itself to the world, the world to itself. Transmits, transports it. Or, consciousness does? Is the I at the border, or is consciousness at the border? But what of body, nervous system?

Give up the idea of trajection?

Consciousness a pendulum—or I or subject as pendulum. Bolted to God by the nerve string which is music. Metaphysical primacy of music: Ardl.

And there *is* a universally shared knowing subject, as he argues?

No, but there's an incestuously shared consciousness: figure of two faces, hourglass!

Mortality yet immortality. Immortality is the pure line drawing, not representing anything. Not mimetic. Expressive. *It* is the vibration, the underlying oscillation.

God is music! God *is* a vibration.

The refusal to be pithy, write beautiful aphorisms. Ugliness and sorrow a part of the philosophical search. So what if they disdain to read you? Your dizziness, visible disturbances cause them nausea. Good. It's better to be alone.

Shell of book.

Shell-shocked brother, sister. When you hear/see the death. Its noisy silence.

*

Georg & Greta, the Translibretto (Is a Labyrinth. Please Don't Get Stuck in It!)
ACTING OUT III
Sehne X
(Castle/asylum on mountainside: two buildings connected by a yellow tower. Derelict garden. Georg sleeps on a couch under a weeping willow tree. Wrists bandaged from recent suicide attempt. Nearby, a slender birch tree; on the other side, a forest edged by honeysuckle bushes w/ pale yellow & white blossoms. By Georg sits Wladek, sorrowful and attentive. From offstage an odd piping sound. Gregor Tristl enters, tall, dark, lanky. He is singing to himself, but his voice makes a whistling, wheezing sound.)

GREGOR
Wladek, hey!

WLADEK
Is she coming?

GREGOR
Oh, my whistling hurt throat would caw like a crow if she came near.

WLADEK
Peel like a bell, it sounds better!

GRETA AS GREGOIRE
I can't stand this. Try theory of speech acts.

GREGOR
Like a promise? *(He looks at his brother Georg, then glances around the garden. Has sudden coughing fit. Exits politely, abashed. Georg mutters, wakes.)*

GEORG
Question?

WLADEK
Exclamation!

GEORG
Frage?

WLADEK
Antwort.

GEORG
Question?

WLADEK
Statement.

GEORG
Frage?

WLADEK
Behauptung.

GEORG
Question?

WLADEK
Declaration.

GEORG
Frage?

WLADEK
(Blah Blah auf Deutsch.)

GEORG
(Confession of his teenage incestuous lust, irresistible yearning. See his poems, prose poems, early plays.)

(Etc., usw.)

GRETA AS GREGOIRE
Wovon man nicht sprechsingen kann —

(Suddenly a loud whistle is heard, then a joyful wheezing.)

WLADEK
It's sis!
(He points to tower, where Gregor is now sticking his head out, nodding, grinning.)

GEORG
Go get her! Tell her to hurry.

WLADEK
Don't torment yourself, bro, I'll bring her!

(Wladek rushes away. Georg tosses agitatedly on couch.)

GEORG
So the son
       act.
          wondrous
Sinister
As night's blot
Outcast's bold mouth
Lust without missing
Its foreign race
            don't linger,
Traitor,
Willing and daring
                 strikes
Tristl
      self graphed,
      grafted
Onto death,
            raised.

(He jumps up.)

With bleeding   backed
once. But now   blue tender
          mirror / sister for dad flower.

(He tears bandages from wrists.)

       plot! To last only   .

(He staggers forward.)

To die by   sleep
   she   hero.   sister,
don't   ideal
    of our   isolation.

(He stumbles to center of garden.)

GRETA
(*offstage*)
Georg! Best brother!

GEORG
    I   this
The licks
        flourish!
Music!   Sister!

(*Greta races in. Georg rushes to her, falls into her arms, collapses.*)

GRETA
Georg! Tristl!

GEORG
Iseult, Gretal!

(*He dies.*)

GRETA
(*ein Gesamtkunstwort*)
Georgnoohnosweetestbrother*lieberBruder*Iamhereyoursisterloverwho
walkedintowaterafteryouoronitLukerlpulledyououtVictorpulledmeb
utwethrewourselfinfrontofabusorsubwaywhowentfirstIwasprecocio
usItaughtyouhowtokissYourthinbutsensualpoutinglipsIGretataught
youhowtokissthefairytalemybrotherisasleepingbeautyYougrowyour
hairlongI'llcutmineshortwe'llconjurematchingsideburnsHowyourco
arsehairprickedmeThenwedodrugsyoushowmehowtoswallowshootS
wallowdon'tspitloveadoremeDon'tbescaredHowwillwesurvivenowt
hatweareorphansorphanedlinesofblownThemamaturnedintoamachi
nethenbrokerepeats*Ihavecommittedacrimetheyarecomingtogetme*Malfun
ctionEvilfunctionsThefathertossedintoaghostonorandorinthemachine
SometimesIfeelsocoldmetallicHavewecommittedacrimeIhavecommit
tedoneThisbodyseeksinfusionensoulmentGeorgawakenSometimesyo
ufeelsocorpseButsourarmpitstenchNotfragrantflowerOrthesmellofyo
urprickOrcomeBrokenmouthMouthinbrow*Inthetwilighttheshadowofth
edeadmanenteredquietlyintothegrievingcycleofhisfamilyandhisstepsrangouti*

81

ncrystalproofendofgreenWoetothestarlikeeyesofhissisterasherinsanitypassedt
opressedovertheontothebrowofherbrotherduringthelastdinnerOrtheeyebro
wsflewofftheforeheadOrpressyourbrowintomypussybrotherOryour
mouthinmymouthoryourcockinmyhandyourtongueonmyneckorhan
donmyribsmineonyourbackoryourribbybackorIwasonceinsideyoulik
eakeyaribormychestwritemynipplesGeorgbutslowdownithurtsIamto
osmalltootightOrmyheaditsskullOrgaveyouheadoryoumeorblewyou
orusawayBlewoffourheadsThedreadfuldrearydaysIkeptmyselffromy
ouwouldnotvisitthismusicOurAustrianinheritanceTheinbornTheunb
oundOIhavecommittedacrimeIrefusedtoseeyouthenyoucamecameto
metoabsolvemedissolvemecomeonmeWecheatedonthetestYourstron
gthighsAsinglemomentRepeatedmomentDidyouforcethisissueIdidn'
tknowhisoryoursIsaidhistowoundyouAreyouwoundedbrotherItwas
NovemberThisisNovemberIsaidNomoreunhappilyyeverafterThejoyth
enightYoucamewhenyoushouldn'thaveThenagainwhenIneededyouY
outhoughtyouwerethesonofChristorGodfromhistenderbrowIghostda
ughterFromhisheadwoundsWewereGodOGeorgHowwillIbearthisN
evertofeelyourbreathonmyneckyourbiteonmybreastyourthickfingersi
nmeYourpoeticcockHowweshudderedGivemebacktheonemomentits
houldlastforeverEternalreverbOnewavevibrationAhbrotherGeorgLis
tenItrocksOursongitslicksItlicksusorweeachotherFatelashesusHowitl
icksusintoonefallenshape—

(She loses consciousness. Gregor rushes in. Wladek enters.)

GREGOR
Wlad! Someone else is coming.

(He stops, stares at Georg and Greta, overwhelmed, sorrowful.)

WLADEK
(frozen, horrified)
Ferdl and Ardl? I won't let them violate this scene. Gregor, help me
lock the gate!

HAAKON
(rushing in)
Ferdek just arrived with other men, I couldn't see who, not a large
number.

(He, too, halts, overcome by what he sees.)

WLADEK
Stay with us and help keep them from your sister and brother, they don't belong!

VICTOR
(outside gate)
Greta! Sister!

WLADEK
Victor? What is he doing here?

VICTOR
Wladek, let us in! Where's my sister?

WLADEK
What, you'd hold her, too? You were always jealous.

LUDVIK
Let us in, Wladek! My brother needs me. My sister.

WLADEK
Oh, you also? Too late, you who could have comforted him!

(Ludvik, Victor and Ferdek break down the gate, run in. Wladek throws himself at them. Knocks down Ludvik, who hits his head.)

LUDVIK
Georg, wait, I'm here!

(He loses consciousness. The others start hitting each other, shouting epithets. After a bit, Ferdek and Victor declaim. Could use Nietzsche and Novalis here. But too high to bother. Greta's last aria. Greta rises slowly, stares at Georg w/ strange ecstasy, moves her mouth and gesticulates but makes no noise at all.)

GRETA
...

(Then she pulls out needle, shoots air into the vein on her arm, dies. Victor cries out, Gregor and Haakon rush forward, Wladek stirs, Ludvik opens his eyes, rubs them, Ferdek calls out.)

FERDEK
No!
But say yes, even to this?
No! Yes! No! Yes! No! Yes!

END / ENDE

*

MUSICAL COMMENTARY
Is it good that the father never spoke?

*

NON-NARRATIVE ARC
In the reverse Pieta, she'd lift her father's body onto the table, green, metallic. Forget that? But remember the Matthäus Grünewald painting you saw as a girl, call him Matthias instead of Antonius? Existential choice of being daily new or being post-. Or suspended, waiting for the subway. Hysterical paralysis, then your brother kisses, wakes you. Haakon is tall with wiry brown hair, a deep voice and aviator shades, he is my brother. I did not know him well, he was a half-brother and younger, I had to imagine him. All the brothers but Georg are half-brothers, have a different father, not hers, who sank upward like a stone. The one choice is stone or else messenger, god, rapid cycler. Moving fast, losing weight, could be a disordered eater like the sister or Gregor. The people won't become your disciples. The father had no male disciples to lift him off, they'd all deserted him/betrayed him/fallen asleep. So the daughter had to do it. Luckily he was very thin by then. Like Duccio's Jesus or a druggy. I will play the keys of his fine ribs, murmurs Greta. Or Grete. She was a talented pianist until the brother impregnated her with his ideas. A messenger can miscarry. Georg's melodrama could sink this book like a stone. Sister paper rock. Sister pupil cock. Grete digressive and *echt* sexual. More experienced than Georg, had many brief affairs, was sexually inventive, even indiscriminate. But wouldn't do it with Georg's *judische Freundin* Else because

anti-Semitic. What should I do with that piece of information? It's enough to make you bulimic. Purging as purist. Isn't Georg's work purgatorial—but private vs. Dante's? Though he says infernal. Don't think about *The Mortal Truth*, it will kill you. As Mina, you broke up with that manuscript, but maybe you'll get back together later. Georg imagined violating and killing the girl, an innocent. Because he felt guilty. You, stony-faced, watch the man or boy expire in front of you. The mother said, She's so cold. Inside you were raging. What attitude to take to expression? Indirection, personas. Ideas fit like masks. Cf. Ensor, Søren. I feel vertiginous. Afraid to walk on stage, do my recital, what if I'm too weak? No one to catch me. Swooning like a hysteric. Sudden death of inspiration. Get back to the question posed by the Holy Spirit. How she seems to be both the sister of the Father (God, Matthias) and the sister of the Son (Jesus, Georg). But if Matthias is Jesus, then his daughter (Greta) can't be the Holy Spirit. But she could be the grandchild / *Enkel* figure in Trakl's poems. The meaning of a name depends on which subtext. How to read Georg. How silver looks different in different stanzas / light conditions. I feel exhausted so I will stop now. Georg rewrote constantly to bring it back to the present moment or else to try to perfect it. Lowered Greta's head onto the table. Verse of self-pity? Eschew it. Yet the *was* was heavy.

*

SWEET NEW THEORY OF MEANING
Meaning depends on contact.

WEDNESDAY MORNING, 3:00 AM THEORY
Meaning depends on conflicts.

WHAT DOES *WEDNESDAY* MEAN?
Wednesday, translation of Latin Mercury day, don't know why.

SWEET NEW STILL
The silence: how it wasn't moving.

CONSEQUENT / TRUTH OF CONSEQUENCES
Fatigue from the operatic inference.

RIGHT NOW
The girl in Scandinavia doesn't write you. The European capital was
Oslo, not Vienna, which is overdetermined. My brother Haakon's
wife Lola doesn't write me either. Georg's sister Grete despised Else,
and Friedrich's sister Elisabeth detested Lou, so Haakon's wife Lola
disdains me—because these turned around are those.

I DESERVE IT
I am a terrible girl.

*

OUR DRUNKEN BOAT
Georg liked Rimbaud, read him to me, then our craft paper got
soaked. *Schwester stürmischer Schwermut/Sieh ein ängstlicher Kahn
versinkt/Unter Sternen,/Dem schweigenden Antlitz der Nacht.* Also on
his bisexual p. 74 it went silver. Greta's brother Lukerl liked young
men such as the thin French-Arab one, olive skin, dark curly hair,
name him Hassan. Olive notebook the building she could build
for her brother in the forest of the city of her head, it would be
whole and simple. Except fragmented and complex. Leaves lit the
window. The question about truth relative to the prose poems.
Correspondence versus something else. Two features rejected which
Greta or Gregoire wants back: correlation of language and world,
importance of first person singular. Lukerl beautiful when young,
and he and Gretal went into the forest. Lemon dots on white shirt.
Reality if and only if poetic. Novalis's magical thinking fights the
analytic death grip. Supposed to redevelop my muscles, but I like
my arms to be '70s slender. Philosophy once an academic discipline.
Leiden nicht. Now it's a toy vessel. A paper boat. Or origami. The seas
of language also folding in.

*

UNNOVALIS (*FIRST DEFACING*)
Ruined on crystal   , high   stranger
From his darkened mouth God named him lament,
As he sank down in his flower
Freed licks, airs   stabbed string
At her breast,
And destroyed her feeling, with   hands foreign,

As he with stammered writing
Silenced night: how verse leaves.

On My Father's (Untold Versions)
Antoine Novels; I'm Novellas; Am Novellas; And My Father's; I'm My
Father's; Am My Father; On No Phallus; And No Veil Is; On No Values;
Grahame's Fall Is; On One Fall As; One New Fall, Loss; Unknown Fall:
Less; I'm Who Fell, Lass; All Unfelt, Last

In My Father's (Stutter Fast Song (Ah))
In dark   er er   ror rots the holy   foreign he
His n   ame from softened mouth: the clocked lament of G   od
As he   hid held   in his   f low   ink
Leapt for   ward his lead, in nigh tly house   of pain.

And My Father's (Why Her Fast Tongue (Aah))
I'm darker ardor wrote her the wholly her-stranger,
was numb from sifted mouth him clang of God,
Dad erring signs blue hint sin,
one blown flower
ad-libbed sung tune I'm night's licks, how-to-suffer.

End Novellas (White Effacing (~B))
                         fremd
     e Knospe

     verstummte   .

                                   *

Abandonment
There will be no word.
There will be no word.
There will be no word.
There will be no word.

Abandon
No word!
No word!

No word!
No need of word!

DEMONSTRATION
1 Sit with your two straight
2 Fingers in your mouth
3 Thumb cocked and
4 Fantasize. A strange
5 Warmth spreads through the
6 Body as a proof.

*

GIVE IT UP?
Georg affected the flaneur when he was Greta in high school and
15. Rolled own cigarettes. This music repellant. They found Gregor
repellent. Insect = incest by transposition of German s (= *Seele*, soul)
and French or Latin c (= *corps*/*corpus*, body/set of writings.) That girl
able to get up and go. Gregor wasn't. Is Greta? While Georg is failing
Latin class.

UTTER LACK OF COSMIC RESONANCE OF GRETA'S FINGERED CHORD
Battle not at Grodek. Dead ones not soldiers. Decline not modernist,
Austrian. Her teeth hurt in infinite ways. All the brothers left Greta
alone. The sister-in-law left Greta alone. The father, the mother.
Deepest intuition of essential solitude of the I. Greta thought to quit
trying to write. Then thought, they have nothing to do with it. But
God? Brief note to the Father. On Him. Her post-it, post id. Stupid
girl.

SELF-DESTRUCTION/SUFFOCATION
Blow us up with her machine? Too long too me. Greta is a need ring.
And too fucking hot in here. Ferdinand far away like summer or
that AP test in Art History. Edvard, Vincent, Ernst, James, Egon—
Should do a section on Egon, he could paint Grete and Georg
half-naked, fondling themselves or each other. Bones, muscles,
strangely patchy skin, obscene curling hair. Egon's sister Grete also
flaming-red-haired, and he painted her. Arguably incest—a theme
of early 20th century German/Austrian lit/life. Never mind that.
Weird exagerrated gestures like that one of Georg's: arms raised and

bent, fingers spread at the sides of his face, palms out, head slightly
cocked.

SOMETHING ON GRETE
I can't picture her now.

*

DOUBT
I don't know what I've been doing.

A stupor put me in its mouth, waited for me to dissolve.

The nerve ends fuzz the logic. Or make it deviant.

Hip bones of philosophical knobs.

Turn this if you want to know something somewhat.

I know that I need to have philosophy.

Incest of philosophy and poetry.

The dark yellow notebook could be something they do together, like
a Euro-twin-size mattress. If I, Greta, also lie around with Lukerl, am
I betraying Georg? What about Gregor, who lives in the next room,
hoping I will feed him crusts and stroke his soft belly? The girl has so
many brothers, each one needs her. Then Victor felt sickly. My head
splitting with the ache, and Greta longed to lie down, but ambition
or virtue thrust her further. But alone.

*

NOT-DARK GRAY-BLUE NOTEBOOK
Metallic fullness. God as the world has arms from shoulders, hot or
cold. But that God is philosophical!

My brother's fascination with the religious ones is my fascination.

I said God was the collection of outlooks, not of things. The infinite
view made of individual views. Benek Esteban said intellect. His

secret idealism. My overt solipsism. It isn't ontological, of being. It is experiential, of encountering. Your world: I accept its existence, but I don't live in it. If our worlds intersect, we're in an intersection set, but I am only in it as it's mine. The problem of other minds is the wrong specialization: epistemic, it's the expulsion. Get back to the philosophy of the tree of life.

God is simply: the force of living?

There is no papa. There is no papa!

But there is beauty. And there is love! They go out with suffering, they all make out.

Greta said, There is only this moment, its truth and I. But it is infused with memory, fantasy, longing, intending. It's not simple, it's complex.

Or how the voice of Ludvig. Of Georg. Of my father.

Or all the moments exist at once, but their character and truth depend on one moment, the present, which keeps changing, becoming another, because it's your locus. Yet which includes/ transmutes them all. The paradox of temporality.

We say, It is true that yesterday it was raining. We don't say, It *was* true that yesterday it was raining. The truth radiates out from the light of now.

But now, for her, God isn't possible. Even as a broken or mad father.

But as a suicide?

Yesterday there was freezing rain. That *is* true.

The desire for certainty is misguided. What's needed is a taste for risk. How you throw yourself into everything with no guarantee. Boldness, even of conviction. But in the *Antlitz* of vulnerability.

The truth is always provisional!

Thus tomorrow my theory itself might change.

The opposition of truth and fragility is false. The truth *is* fragility. Fragility is the truth. My fragile brother!

No norms which could be crutches. My poor outsider brother Ludvik, wishing to join in. Versus my brother Georg, choosing to opt out.

Every morning, the possibility of the abyss of the elevator shaft outside the door. Or how my room became a grim forest. Or how the pond a danger.

But God.

How can I love God when I don't believe in God?

How can I serve God when He doesn't exist anymore?

But I still feel Him!

But I love, serve, feel my brother! My father.

How it spills outward in its necessity that has no logic.

And knocked the glass of water over, just to prove it!

But love includes that you disagree. So love without the perpetual yes?

I wrote, Wrestling ontology.

I shouted, Ishmael!

While my brother dutifully followed our father up the mountain, played Isaac. Wanted his I to be slain.

But if I translate him? Carry, bear his dead body? To move or carry from one place to another: *The girl monk translated the holy relics to their new shrine. Die Mönchin!* To remove to heaven without a natural death. *By faith, the father was translated, that he should not see death.* To cause to lose sense or recollection: to entrance. *Georg was translated by the blow to the head he received, being unable to speak for the next minutes.* Years? Then he lay on top of me, made me into a silent echo with his hands.

God, the godhead, is neither the world nor my independent I. For my I is not independent, and the world is not worthy of adoration. And God must be worthy of adoration—

But isn't the world worthy of adoration?

Or why must God be worthy of it?

Ah, Georg!

God is not nature, God is not fate, God is not a character or person or being.

God is inspiration?

God is the feeling, the force?

The form?

God is not certainty.

The form is not certainty.

The truth as conditional—vs. the truth-conditional account of truth.

Proffering, responsiveness vs. reference, correspondence.

His ribby back, his soft smooth faintly lime-scented skin. But he felt leper.

The language isn't God either? The language is the God-vehicle?

God, the word, the spirit = God, the expression, the girl.

But if you lose the ability to find the expression? To infuse it?

There has to be a brother for the sister!

Or how the feeling surges, gathers you up, carries you along.

Or the sister is the expression, expressivity. The word is vitality, life, but the spirit is emotionality, feeling.

Why doesn't the Scandinavian girl write to me?

Her darker skin, her cropped hair, her supernipples.

Constant adjustment of the clothing, no temperature that lasts, stays comfortable.

It isn't necessary or right to feel comfortable!

Every day, the reinvention of the world, how you inflate it through a speech balloon.

Ergo the creation, that fairy tale.

In which the language, too, must be reinvented.

Truth and meaning rise and fall together.

If I could have found the new *syntax*, would I thereby have saved my brother?

But I couldn't find it!

How the grammar is a matter of life or death.

The structure, form of living, of the world.

The shared grammar of the poetics and the metaphysics.

The transfigured phrase, clause, sentence?

Now my head feels too exposed. So I put on my black hoodie.

I think, Should I grow my hair like my brother's earlier or shave it like his later?

The I that is entered by the other I's. The first person singular not simple, pure. Interpenetration, openness, but still an isolation, metaphysical solipsism. But impacts, connections, affections. Thus no monad. So then how is it isolated? And aren't there shared aspects?

The first person singular is the sibling I. The sibject!

But that will not bring your brother back.

Then I think, Were we not from a different planet? Abandoned here, orphaned?

Alien, *Fremde, Fremdling*.

Suddenly the

                                        *

THE?
—

                                        *

DISTRACTION
Month of silence.

MEMORIAL
This was the day he
                      came knocking on her
                                        chest or brow or pupils.

94

The man's mouth ironed smooth her brow,
                              the girl's long hair
                              rained onto his ribs.
Therefore today I   do not die or live here.
Undo   glue   gun   function.

*

SHATTER PROOF (GRAY NOTEBOOK MANQUÉ)
It's been too long to remember how to tongue-kiss. She would
like to sleep now for a fairy tale. Wide face, small blue eyes, pouty
mouth, rapacious nostrils: sibling doubles. Georg will be played
by Peter Sarsgaard, Grete/Greta by Kate Winslet—no, by Kristen
Stewart w/ dyed dirty blonde hair: *Twilight* reboot! Dirty blondes
have more pain! Also she looks slightly like me. But isn't Peter too
old for her? Ryan Gosling or Dane DeHaan, then? Either way, girl
gets the stronger chin. Forget that all these actors are prettier than
the real Trakls. But that last exclamation point was false. It's to fill
the mouth in the brow, the brow in the mouth. You could swallow
one at a time, every moment rechoose it. Because of horror. Georg's
friends heralded his weird poems, while her dissonances did not get
heard. Poor grammar. To swallow this draft is to commit suicide?
Stillness hovered over the book as a good. Two patterns clashed,
created sexual tension. Brother and sister in a tent in the backyard.
Or playing handball in front of the building. Tawdry garden. The
Japanese garden needed weeding, so the mama. Taught of beauty.
Momentary warmth, excitement. No pain in the shine? Eyeliner
on a Japanese girl. Extremism of Greta's metaphysics expressed in
chromatic power chords beyond the Tristan chord. Sexual allure of
12 year-old boy indicating nostalgia or perversion. How far should
this go? Connection between blurred vision and sharper hearing,
but the ringing drowns out everything. Something drugged things.
Warping of the LP on the turntable. Truth needle and the beauty of
sleeping for a longer time, as through puberty. Many people bring
their ponds here. Only Greta's is the immature idea of Narcissus
metaphysics, instrumental solipsism. The world is my performance,
my interpretation. Ergo something is the score? Knowing the score
vs. scoring vs. being scored. And scoring vs. scoring vs. scoring. Take
it to the limit. Like she slow-danced to the Eagles or Bread. W/ the
camp counselor Lee, dark gold long hair, gentle voice, jutting hip

bones. *You are very mature for your age.* Then did nothing. A field of shattered dying soldiers is completely different. Still, she wanted to die. Because it wanted to. The suffering persisting. No consolation of expression of the age, its character. No such grandiosity. But sight-reading or scoring the whole world for *yourself* is truly selfish. This informal proof has no line numbers or inference rules, yet these notes reverberate. Which was to be devastated.

Metaphysical Simple
Wrote a prose poem, feel a little better now. Don't feel like dying.

But Why?
But why is there no music? Did my brother swallow it all?

*

Insight
The magical bluish light on the tablets. They could swallow you.

Enter Haakon
Last night or this morning, realizing who her brother Haakon is. He is a prince and a good, loyal brother, as in a German or Scandinavian fairy tale. But I don't like it when he puts his mouth on mine, because my mouth is Georg's. With Victor, it's more complicated. A history to be turned into story.

BTW, I Don't Look Like Grete, I Look Like Charlotte Gainsbourg, Who's Smarter
Victor is the young man or manchild who's Asian but Slavic, from the eastern part of Russia or the former Soviet Union. So not really Chinese, more like Siberian-Mongolian. Small yet long wideset slanted eyes, short dark hair, dainty features, blemished skin. A short slight body. Tenderness with grand ambitions. He is the brother to whom Greta is closest. They are spitting images of each other, they trade spit when they kiss, they spit images at each other, they imagine their spit making strings that bind them together for all eternity. Once Victor spat on Greta when he felt furious at her because she was leaving, going outside to play with a boyfriend such as Carlos. Then he, Victor, groveled and cried and beat his concave boyish chest in remorse. Did she, Greta, forgive him? Didn't she?

Stay tuned.

TUNEFUL
Looney toons, lunatic tunes, Heraclitus' tuning, Greta's tune,
Ferdek's tune-up, Georg's tune-in, drop-out.

IN GERMAN
Stimmen means tune, also be correct, right, true. And voices. I think
this needs to be autotuned for the LP. But life is live performance.

WORRY
If I move to that guy's chair, will I develop his cough? As he was
leaving, he forgot to cover his mouth.

WORRY #2
If I move to his chair, will I develop his syphilis? As he was leaving,
he forgot to zip up his fly.

PROPHECY
The bad noises coming from the chair: creaks of foreboding.

LOGIC
She found it hard to believe in that. I mean, the rain. She did not
believe in it. Therefore it was not true, and she did not say it.

DELUGE
They were on the boat, they were all alone, the boat was drunk, they
were brother and sister. She touched his ribcage. He said, I invented
you. She said, I fought my way out of you. There was no God to steer
them or make it quit raining.

NIGHTLIGHT
The arc of their story does not protect them. The rain remaining a
perpetual temptation. In the cellar or in the tower or in the closet or
the attic or the bedroom they had to share until she was given her
own room. He wanted the nightlight on, she wanted it off. Then
what happened?

CONFESSION #3
It's been a while since I've read Novalis, i.e. since I've talked to Victor/Vincenzius.

MAGICAL IDEALISM
The name Novalis was also a fairy tale. Once it lost another girl wisdom, like Sophie of Edvard.

EMPATHIC AS I AM
Georg did not believe in poetic confessions; he believed in abstract expressions. Articulations of universal feelings/states. Or anyway impersonal ones. What does that mean? Greta said, I feel, therefore this is. Too self-conscious? But expression vs. description. The metaphysical/poetical subject shows itself even when it doesn't say itself. Georg said, Friedrich's late hymns. Greta said, Anton's early tunes. Then thin ice on the pond. Theory cracks or theory of cracking. Silver extremities.

THE SIBLING SUBJECT
The sibject. Then shame of neologism. Or of its logic.

CORRESPONDENCE THEORY
The boy fact, the girl true sentence. Boys are less verbal? For a while, meanings seemed ghostly, immaterial. Absence of a theory of incarnation in semantics. The minor version of correspondence is compatible with idealism, perspectivism, subjectivism, aspectualism, first personalism, even entailed by them. I refuse to stop now. Yet I never move forward. Unresponding theory. Our co-dependent pond is too smooth. Or too rough.

*

BLUISH PALE VERY GRAY NOTEBOOK
Consciousness as illumination. Bright gray like the sky today. One sign of the rightness of my vision!

The viewing activity: is viewing passive? It is not passive!

But consciousness isn't the medium of the swinging subject, it's too partial. The medium is energy, electricity.

Georg's electric touch!

The swinging subject = the sibject.

The sibject!

Incest semantics! Incest metaphysics! But also first person singular.
The relativity of it. Which, strictly, can't be said.

The subject and object fuse to become one sibject. The glowing
sibject. There are others. But also all are one—

Have incest here! I mean, finally explain it. But I can't, too distracted!

All consciousness is individuated and impure.

Consciousness as flower on stem of I, subject, sibject.

If sibjects, then what are the parents?

The father wilting like a flower. The father vanishing into the floral
wallpaper.

They said, Why don't you be philosophical about it? She said, I can't,
I am hysterical.

I am impure, cries Greta. With pride and shame. Does that mean I
am not precious? Fine, I don't want to be precious.

In the middle ages, I meant purity.

Reread that slim book aka poem, how it is a pubescent labyrinth.
How the father loses the daughter too early, versus the inverse.

Pearlescent, pubescent. Scent. Ferdi said he had a good sense of
smell. I, Greta, say I have a bad sense of small.

Scale is everything. Last night the cellist played one. I mean many. I
listened to Bach's cello sonatas.

Consciousness a sonata? A solo is a sonata that is not a solipsist.

Consciousness is a solo. Consciousness is solo. It is single and a pearl.

If there were no pain, irritation, there would be no self-consciousness. In joy, there is loss of self. In pain, the self layers up, hardens.

There has to be suffering for there to be a soul, thus taught our Fedushka.

There existed no pain until there was the mental anguish of feeling inferior and ambitious, wanting to be more. Desire for the apple not because it was beautiful and shiny and they were hungry, as in a fairy tale. Rather, because it was the better self. Will to power? Will to flower? But flower ≠ pearl.

Without the sin/pain, no forming of the jewel: the shiny stone of self.

Georg's stoniness, Ferdinand's stoniness, Greta's rockiness.

Die Welt ist alles, daß Juwel ist. The world is all that the jewel is.

I don't mean Jew, do I? The issue of the Jew, for me and my brothers. Abstract, concrete.

The Virgin Mary was a Jew, so was the Frigid Maria—no, the Rigid Marya, our mother.

Jewel a gem. *Jules et Jim!* And Jeanne Moreau. The threesome like Tristan, Mark, Iseult. The French New Wave vs. the sweet new style. Last night, talked to the French lady from upstairs, later read more about Dante.

The tweet new style. But I refuse to do that!

The sweet nu: stale? Is it good for the jewels?

The jewels are also men's balls in dirty slang. That's disgusting. I wish Greta hadn't recalled that.

Riding the new wave. Vertigo sans nausea. First I wrote nostalgia. Whirling.

The whirl is all that is the case. The pearl is all that is the case.

Gem: bud, jewel. The budding flower! The yellow flower? Or the bluish light gray one? Could there exist a pale gray flower?

Jew + el. Elevated, elevation. Elohim. God on the New York metro!

Jewel derives from plaything, of play. Like playing with yourself and being chastised by your mother or the governess. Or playing with the boys, or with the big brothers.

Where are these thoughts coming from? I have to think them, maybe I don't want to think them! But can't consciousness just detach, watch a thought pass, be a view?

A pearl is not a stone. My brothers were stony, while I was hard and cold but never a stone.

Gem from *geminate*: to make or become doubled or paired, as w/ a brother. Or gem as type of a size bigger than brilliant. Such as genius!

Ferdl craved a secretary to copy his sentences, I long for a typist to type up my notebook. Maybe Stig could do it when his wrist heals. I would give him long breaks to invent guitar riffs. I would come up with licks. We could be a sibling duo like The Carpenters or The Fiery Furnaces.

Georg could've played with me, but he is gone.

Should the same star who plays Greta play Gregoire? Or should Gregoire be e.g. Léa Seydoux or Nick Stahl? Both have suitably flared nostrils. But no, Nick should play Stig! Metaphysics of casting!

34% of us say our dream job is to be an actor. Greta read that.

All the levels of the subject swing, not simply consciousness. The moving I, the wandering I, the veering I, the roving I, the vagrant I, the vagabond I.

But why is it the same I? Metaphysics of personal identity.

Sudden heavy tread upstairs. The aunt of Ferdl Thurstan, who lets the room to 18 year-old Gretl. Greta went to Berlin to continue her studying. Of philosophy or the piano. That is certain. Ardl Sebastian is the elder brother of Ferdl. He will never publish me, he looks down on me because I am female. Or else he's jealous of my phrases and ideas. He also lives in our boarding house in Wilmersdorf. *Wilmer* means will + fame! Ardl, Ferdl and Gretl are all very ambitious. So is Lukerl. So was Wlad! Be careful that the males or brothers do not keep you down.

The brother is supposed to carry or keep or guard or protect you like the father did, I mean the treasure. The pearliness.

Wandering vs. oscillating. Obsessing over—

Stop it, Greta! Don't assent to bad thoughts such as a feeling of betrayal by a brotherly lover like Wladek. He, not Greta, did the leaving. Meanwhile they kept the secret from Georg, who was in the possessive mental case. Was it. His world.

Greta is brutal. Hostile. Juvenile.

But a better part of me detaches. The divided consciousness proves the divided I.

The I itself a labyrinth. Then what/who enters it: consciousness? Or the first person singular is really double, one I entering the other? Or a multiple: a disordered n-tuple. Or, self the labyrinth, I the pilgrim? Then is the maze unicursal or multicursal? I.e. can mistakes be made? The fate question once again.

The thing in the center isn't the thing in itself, *der Ding an sich*. It's Christ as double. Unless his sister.

The string theory of the nerves, and the pitches wading through the window. I did not will or choose them, they were thrown at me. It's easy to feel thrown and to turn anxious. Then the theory of the maze doesn't help you to escape.

Paranoia, dread, loneliness, megalomania, melancholy, apathy.

The philosophers have bad temperaments. Usually they're not blessed like Manuel Kurt or Benek Esteban. Perhaps it is only the systematizers who can be calm, not the systematically nervous ones.

The viewing I is conditioned by features of the particular self, e.g. its temperament. So never perfectly abstract, pure. It's veridical because it affirms or denies, like the title of my still uncomposed Russian novel, *Yea and Nay*. Thus it wills.

I am so hungry, I need to take a break. I would like a Bratwurst, please.

In Russian *Brat* means brother. My brother Ludvik, who admired Lev and Feodor, fantasized about going to Russia. He passed through Oslo on his way to the fjords but did not have sex with a shining starlike girl. *Ludvik* means famous warrior.

In Wilmersdorf, I—Greta unless Gregoire—studied German, and my German improved, but my will did not become famous, and I did not become famous, although I willed my fame. But that was before.

*

REMEMBER THAT LSD TRIP, SAYS ONE GUY
I don't want to talk about it, thinks Greta. Hallucinations like Georg. Negative spirographs: white on ballpoint-pen blue sky. Language breaking, snapping. Scratched mirror of language. Panavision vs. monovision. Schizovision? Germany won, Austria wasn't playing. Greta played w/ Georg, who was Austrian like Ludvik, *nämlich* of mixed descent. Haakon was Scandinavian, Gregor Czech-Jewish,

Victor Slav-Asian. So make Greta *echt* Austrian, i.e. everything, and from Gotham City. Pure = impure in the Austro-Hungarian Empire State, but never mind that. The father tongue beckons. Georg also speaks it. Inherited vs. inserted like a Metro card. *I probably would still go to most places. It has an elevated train, so it's weird.* From up there, I could see the river, think about the Eastern front. First stop in Brooklyn: Galicia. That horror's really obvious like a baby blanket. Lately Greta hasn't been sleeping, and when sleeping, has been having bad dreams. The one about trying to get back home, but the public transportation leads you astray. Private transport such as ecstasy with a forbidden God or girl. But the word *transport* is decayed, grotesque, horrific. The word stabs her head. Why I am afraid. I forget the names of the videos I meet at the parties. Also she was freezing. Then the throat hurts from breathing or declaiming. Recitative. Musical outlet w/ wrong voltage. A risk of travel. The meaning is the second layer, a skin tone. The bat signal doesn't help. I was scared of them like Christian Bale. He could play Haakon. No, how about Clive Owen? Joseph Gordon-Levitt would play Victor. Except he isn't Asian. *Doch*, he's so-called Semitic. But the problem of age-inappropriateness. Likewise when Ludvig and Gregor get cast. Whatever. Greta's lack of discipline created a blemish on her face like the mark of Cain, only on her left cheek, not her brow, because she never turned it. It was the other one, the one of the other. Pain, love and anger towards at least one brother. Now trade all the brothers for the one father. He could be your superbrother, overbrother, *Überbruder*.

SADNESS
I think this is the beautiful Schubert sonata. Franz like Georg dying young.

BEAUTY
I think that was the sad Schubert sonata. Georg like Franz staying pretty.

SUSCEPTIBILITY
The way she rearranges her papers inside my neck causes it to hurt inside its throat.

PROPHECY
Staring at the open and shut case, trying to let the blue light burn out
your eyes. Easier to hear if blind. That already wrote me.

WORD PROBLEM
Will I come back later? Will Greta?

BAD GIRL
They died, the father and the brother, when you did not nurse them
like a sister in a white outfit of snow. Or in an X-rated fit.

*

SWITCH
Last night the dream that her brother was taking her from behind.
One hole, then the other. Disgusting because it was Gregor, not
Georg. Then Egon Schiele depicted their angular fuck, because *he's*
compulsive, too. Berlin the very pale gray notebook, not the blue
octavo. But bluish with cold or dead lips. This morning she was cold
and dead, therefore the world was. Does it matter whose hands they
were? No condom. Father's face a floating reproach. Her long hair
wrapped around them, her brothers. Edvard Munch's sister. Wisdom
in the form of a girl roams the streets lamenting, unheeded. In Berlin
ich bin heiß / *I am hot* means just: I am feeling turned on, sexy—but
Greta wasn't. The building surges up. It was to her too cold. Memory
vs. memorial. Bluish pale gray day of rain. Forty minutes of deluge.
Never went back there. The bluish very pale gray notebook is the
condom. Also thin like a teenage girl aka novella. Thin-skinned.
Ice blue milk. She's so thin, cried out someone admiringly. An old
woman walked with a cane. Her young male orderly pushed her
wheelchair next to her, in case she needed it; he seemed tender. It
was beautiful because I did not matter to it at all.

*

VERY LIGHT GRAY BLUISH VERY NOTEBOOK
The subject that says *I think* affirms; it is the veridical subject. The
thinking subject thinks the thought that is being thought in me. But
the I might not affirm it. So the thinking subject is not always first-
personal, it could be third-personal? But then the veridical subject's *I
think* is a lie? Or what does *I think* mean?

Viewing x as a vs. being *aware* of viewing x as a vs. *affirming* viewing x as a.

The thinking subject can think two thoughts at once, even contradictory ones. Can the averring subject aver them? Yes!

Alternation between a bad thought and my censure of it, vs. never affirming the thought at all, so it becomes mere content. *It* affirms *P*, although *I* don't. It stays alien to me. But how? Is it part of my I?

This is a phenomenology of mentality.

I have been throwing around terms like I, consciousness, thought, subjectivity, view with no rigor. I have been terribly sloppy!

Greta likes sloppy sex.

The I of consciousness gets lost in the I of self. Of subject?

Why am I saying subject and not sibject? Or do I mean them to be synonymous?

I, Greta, am so undisciplined, so unintelligent now. When my brother died, my brilliance died with him.

Furthermore, I can't keep up with my notebook, I mean typing it. I need a secretary like Joanie from *Mad Men*, who's smart, witty, sexy and curvaceous in her push-up Maidenform brassiere.

Greta's ivory white slightly padded bra when 13 years old! The Maidenform of judgment. Girlish form of truth.

My brother Lukerl said form of life, I think he took it from Ferdl, who was our tutor when we were young, until he ran away from our mama's parochialism in disgust.

I keep neglecting Lukerl, who was supposed to be Georg's rival for my sisterly affections. But I have just turned 19 years old, I am living in Berlin and still merely betrothed to Ferdl Thurstan. Furthermore, my brother Georg cannot be dead yet. For he has not yet come after me because I wouldn't visit him, and forced himself on me and arguably impregnated me, such that later I would suffer a terrible abortion, being Grete.

Thurstan must not be confused with Tristan, which is an alias for my brother Georg.

The alias for Ferdinand/Ferdl is Ferdek because he has Polish pretensions, thinks he is of Polish royalty, disdains the Germans. Also it sounds like King Mark, so it is very clever.

They said, Quit saying how smart you are! You are greedy for praise. You should show it, not say it. She replied, Then you'll accuse me of showing off. Then she did that thing with her tongue, moving it around in her mouth, under her lips. Then they fumed, because they were sexually frustrated.

My alias is Iseult, which does not sound like Greta, but never mind that. I want to do musical innovations, new soundscapes and formal structures!

My hair smells like a German opera.

The Greta and Georg music to go with the libretto; I keep forgetting to compose it because of philosophy.

I keep failing to settle on the title. *Greta & Georg*? *Torment and Insult*? *True Tale of Incest*?

I am a dreamy adolescent girl with a musical future. Like Grete, the sister of Gregor in that anorexic novella.

That could be another opera: *Veer and Wander. Variation. The Forfending.*

Once I wrote a notebook called *Titular*, it was a nominal poem consisting solely of titles of possible poems. Possibility is an important category in philosophy. I don't think that Ferdl worked out his attitude to necessity and possibility. I don't know what I think yet about metaphysical fatalism.

Please, Greta! Get back to work.

Suddenly I feel lazy. Although that is the only one of the seven sins from which I do not chronically suffer.

But right now I feel too lazy to think, so I decide to practice my music.

Listen:

II. brother or sister

IF TO RESTART WITH A BANG (BULLETIN)
Madness of rustled. The woman wore a beige leprous carpet. French
as Baudelaire or homework. Feels lonely. Shouldn't I have talked
to him? *Feel like you're the only.* It won't work when the syllables
refuse to lie down, be the sister. Flits around, is impersonal. The
best emergency cave. So he was in Bellevue for a long. Coughed-
up line reading. Opened her chest, pulled out a gender. Portrait
of the artist by a cosmos. Named Milena? No, she's in that other
fortress. Realized the translation. Too flowery, not modern. Twilight
fingered petals. The wound is all the fall is. Floor shudders with
blows, intentions. The all fell apart, pink and orange cardboard
dollhouse. Going too far to still be a. Practicing the other language
doesn't. Veiled disappearances, e.g. father accent. The daughter a
parking ticket: orange, white, wet, flung away. Don't realize what.
Basic French vocabulary. *Desolée.* Half the conversation died, was
muted. Mutability of blue jeans. Free shortening. The poem bunched
down around the ankles, dragged on the sidewalk, frayed, dirtied.
Messing, messing with, messing in, messing around, messing up.
Ready to quit being myself now, instead be. Key copied. Did not
help to move, the movement a. Not a stunt but stunted. Because the
bookbag hung too heavy. Crashed. Made a long sentence sh.

SIGHT & SOUND
On Richard Wagner's ring finger
Skull or star or skulk or stare in a Trakl opera
I said, Brother, can't we write one?
But my brother was precocious
Left her grasping at thin airs
Expressionist like white
Of eyes or face or an icy mountain
Alban Berg in plaintive song
Singed or broken
The notes defy the keys
So there still is mystery
Of must that's unforeseeable
Trakl/Amsel (he is his poem) and Gretal walked in the high wood
Then Marcus gave a freebee w/ Frisbee
Scratched the liquid surface
Of their faces' book, while

Back-lit, the siblings shunned it
Fused, it sounds fugal, seeks the fugitive
Escapes by sound wave
Slapped the drink down the ink
Clicked into places like face down
In the forced field of conscription's
Inscription. Encryption, or in a crypt. But the
Matte pix of the death stones stayed black, bordered,
Inscrutable. Overexposed
Or over, ex-, post-
Psst, whispered this
But she didn't hear

SUDDEN DEATH
Because cold or fled. The strands of things hit flying.
Light turning to a turnstile. My big brother Georg murmured,
Put the German quote here: *Ein Toter besucht dich. Aus dem*
Herzen rinnt das selbstvergossene Blut und in schwartzer Braue
nistet unsäglicher Augenblick; dunkle Begegnung.
I, his sister, transmuted: A dead man visits you. Out of
the hurt sound runs the flash-flooding blue tone in swarthy brows
nixing unsayable eyeblinks; dark ill beckoning.
Haakon said, Never suicide. Or held the dark thing back
through sound's syllabic excess, egress, but she, egregious,
brought it close like his crumpled brow, his eyelids, kissed it.
Melancholia blew on branches. *Tochter, Toter.* Totter, clatter.
His nasal whine went up in smoke. Her legs uncrossed the box.
Tears whipped the face, wiped the present
tense to cleanse it. Virgin versification, as faked
transfiguration. The wandering of buzzards. Ink black milkshake
with no cosmic or historic significance. Girl's drink, grasp the
straw. Solipsistic slipknot.

EP
The thing was at an angle, so it spilled
I sat in the past, did not understand the Chinese female syllables
His ferocious spittle hat!
They laugh and do weird moves on the jungle gym
Glee presses the sustain pedal

The camouflage pants sat down too close to me, I tried not to
Think war
The first one of the world, or the perpetual machine
Young skinny umber boy's grass-green and sun-yellow t-shirt,
He eyed me with superiority
The new bike lanes are painted in the wild green of Vincent's
Japanese self-portrait
Actually not as brilliant, more the milky green of that other painting
Chino-Latino white sneakers
Moved and felt good
Words need to circulate
I was a bad desk or delivery
Girlboy who'd read Joe and feel euphoria
For who knows how long?
The vagrancy of cloud moves
The other woman did high kicks over
My retro baggage
I still look younger is maybe when it's time to end it
The whole gray day ate like a beggar to the siren
Armless motions
The whole note, immobilized, rests—
But no!
Refuse to end like that. The day barked and chased a different
version of itself. There don't have to be sentences, only splashes.
@leaves, leashes, day jobs.
The sleepers as dark splotches on a semi-abstract painting. The
visuals low-slung, sexy. I could end it like this. I'm taking it easy like
you are. Said the derelict. The other guy grinned, leaned forward and
read. This went on longer than I thought.

BLUISH PALE GRAY SLIGHTLY NOTEBOOK TRANSPOSED INTO PROSE POEM
Tried to seduce all the older men, but too *aggressive* to have a real
mentor. Ergo unpublished. Meaning has its own graph, the sibling
of the truth graph. The brother theory traveled up through the body,
put pressure on the lungs, hit the throat. Meaning does not have
its own graph, it's the third axis of the truth graph, gives it depth,
the third dimension. The negative side correlation, simple and
ascetic. The positive side implications, complicated and excessive.
Denotation vs. connotation, reference vs. sense, thing vs. way of

thinking, about or from or over it. The philosophers argued: truth-conditional semantics vs. conceptual-role semantics. Cf. mimesis vs. excursus. But I, Greta, do not care for that. I want to have my fact and eat it, too. I said, Give me a bite of the fruit. Hallucinated a black snake swallowing itself. Girls also kill themselves with nooses. The trick is to know how to grasp the right end. A man or manly girl uses a gun. Georg failed at it. Then he wanted to save his coke and snort it, too. Grete high on Chopin, Liszt, the Russian Romantics, I on Schopenhauer, lists, the German Romantics. Living in Berlin, I slept with a young man. Brother or boyfriend? Grete's infant formula stillborn, Greta's formula still infantile. How to include the spaces? Rest cures or pauses in the music. The picture theory need not be facile correspondence. Although the meaning world must shimmer. Classical like semantics and/or modernist like music. At 18, Grete or Greta fled from Georg in Vienna to Berlin, to study piano earnestly. Then her father died.

THE MUSIC DIDN'T STOP
A gesture named Christoph Mac Clay broke some LPs, she couldn't bring herself to. Clay implies mortal. Grooves of blackness, white sleeves' straitjacket, scratch and spin. Yellow jacket one ecstatic way Georg taught her drugs, while Victor, scared, played pinball. Or Pong or ping pong, which he won. Dashes, beeps. Shag haircuts and carpets, suede chokers. Can't confine yourself to one brother, are a nymphomaniac like Glenda Jackson in that movie. Even the awkward boys. Her tongue kept escaping from her mouth. This music discursive, should be recursive. Unable to write cheerful round voluptuous feminine script, but it doesn't require big tits to be popular. Elsewhere, pure bells and a mad girl in white w/ a bandaged wrist, a perfumed microphone. To manipulate the tones or shapes of space w/ your Intendo. Searching, but also for what to search for. Hid under the tree, recalled the swing, the weeping willow. Time a signature. The inner hear has two labyrinths, one hard, one soft.

*

THE BROTHER VARIATIONS
1   The stranger was the brother, lay in bed weak, no longer protective. Our wound bleeding. She did not wish to play with him.

Or did only when he was Georg, not Victor. Gregor in love with the high-strung instrument of his sister. Her strands of hair. How she danced to disco music. Victor? Father's face dissolved foreign city's shadows. Mother's brittle jewelry. Corpses drag themselves across rosy carpets. *Rose in Bloom.* Tone of rose in his writing.

2   Haakon tall, wiry, generous. Gregor tall, skinny, dreamy. Georg, of medium height, strong, sorrowful. Lukerl, of medium height, angular, irritable. Victor, short, thin, cheerful. The boys/brothers as comics, books. The father as faded flower.

3   The father/brother Antoine/Antonius: tall, lanky, melancholy. I want to look like Montgomery Clift who looked like my father. Or we felt like him because of heavy eyebrows. My brother wants me to look like Elizabeth Taylor with Monty in that movie, be sophisticated yet sweet, girlishly warm, sisterly or as if a young mama, and comfort him.

4   Father and daughter shared a (type of) mother. Remote like a lunar body. Cool temperature, bare table, mourning ceremony. Father-daughter wanderers. Guilt of father flower. Is that sin original? It's classic. Then he left her. The *Leaves Trilogy.*

5   Mother rigid at the table. Brother frantically hopeful. Father a negative space. Unwritten Trakl poem. The girl did not ask to be excused, could never be forgiven. Banished herself. The one who forces himself on you, the one who comforts you, the one who protects you, the one who defends you, the one who builds for you, the one who pines for you, the one who admires you, the one who neglects you, the one who abandons you. There were no stone steps, but a cement stairwell, a metallic elevator. Too much to order, so she embraced disorder, opened her mouth to it.

6   The girl tomboyish though delicate, should've gotten a prick. Although she doesn't know how to climb a tree. At night down the cliff, the brothers could reclimb it. A sister is alone at the limit. Ambiguity does not depersonalize. Fantasy of universality in Georg's ear. In Greta's, willful idiosyncrasy.

7   Haakon put his brotherly book next to hers, the books held hands and wandered into the dark forest/maze. Haakon and Greta. Georg and Gretl. Victor and Gretal.

8   Leafy trees wiped the night sky blackboard clean of chalky stars. The inner ear inflammation heard ruthless ringing. Read that book about labyrinths. I feel so cold. The brother Victor yanked her up out of the wet snow where she had been lying facedown, drowning. Would the snow sentence, its truth, lead you out?

9   Lukerl missed Georg by three days, philosophy missed Greta, I mean Gregoire, by three moments or months or yearbooks. Is it too late for a *tractatus*? But the cursed words. Lukerl shook his head, not like the other brothers. Ditto she. The thesis on meaning as antithesis to mourning. Or meaning and melancholia? Clarity hurt the poem but helped the prosaic. The music sleepwalks. Greta is afraid to wake it up.

*

ALL THAT WAS IS THE CASE
Once upon a time, the father dies in 1910. Brother and sister intimate. Mother a taut contour. Two paragraphs later, Grete runs away to Berlin, attends a master class with Dohnányi. Meets Langen, brother of the publisher, in Wilmersdorf pension, he the pension lady's nephew, thirty-three years older than Grete. Had the papa protected her from the intensity of Georg? Two pages later, Grete weds longing, gives up composition, her concert pianism. Georg back in Vienna, haunted by memories. Feels he killed the father by loving the sister. Dissolute period, failed job attempts. Writes to Grete, who admonishes him; awaits her in Salzburg in 1913, she won't come. November 1913, sister crisis. She spurns him, his letters. Resolves to get pregnant by her husband. Georg despairing. Grete pregnant by one or the other. Her miscarriage connotes a curse. Drug-fed abortion? Georg guiltier still. Grete bleeds danger. Georg goes to her in Berlin-Wilmersdorf. Back to Innsbruck, paints self-portrait. War. Tries to get money to help sister. June or July, receives Ludwig's money. Is sent to the Galician front. Suicide November 3, 1914, age 27. Grete increasingly impoverished, indebted, addicted, transient. Her suicide comes three notebooks later, September 22, 1917, at her

new address; she's 26.

WHAT GRETA ASKS HERSELF
Is this professional suicide?
Is this amateur suicide?
Is this creative suicide?
Is this intellectual suicide?
Is this financial suicide?
Is this slow suicide?
Is this social suicide?
Is this spiritual suicide?
Is this metaphysical suicide?
Is this nominal suicide?
Is this linguistic suicide?
Is this textual suicide?
Is this visual suicide?
Is this aural suicide?
Is this attempted suicide?
Is this faked suicide?
Is this failed suicide?
Is this metasuicide?
Is this the suicide of suicide?

GESAMTSELBSTMORD
~~Commitsuicidekillyourselflayhandsonyourselfdoawaywithyourself
makeawaywithyourselfputanendtoyourselfdiebyyourownhandslayy
ourselfslaughteryourselftakeyourownlifetakeyourselfoutdoyourselfi
noffyourselfenditall~~

THE SUICIDE PARADOX
How is suicide possible? How can what kills be identical to what is
killed? Is it two parts of the same I? Or does the subject step to the
side, become another? To turn on yourself, double-back on yourself,
like the self-swallowing snake. But it never swallows its own head,
that isn't possible. Further, the eye does not see itself. So in suicide,
the I does not slay itself? Thus the bare idea of suicide is a fraud? Is
impure?

*

Aus Satz Theorie, a Poem

Outcast set of leprous facts, alien sentences
Mirror theory of *leper* and *repel*
It's psychological or logical, semantic
or psychosomatic; it's a staging. But
a brother martyr will still kiss you
Principality of sufficient unreason's liason
Then Gretel's cleverness falls off the poem
Dead skin tone poem, black mark on white cheek, as
if each sibling were Cain *and* Abel. Mixed *Geschlecht*
And mix of different meanings, propositons
The androgyne is persecuted as dregs. But that's not why
to leap; it's to do the movement like music
Or the typological, set composition
Or the unutterable, mystical theorem
Cf. *Aussatz*

Raised Dots (Prose Poem Transposed into Light Gray Notebook)

Shared his milk with me, did not demand my birthright.

Too sweet? The sweeter girl, a ghost, appeared off-register. Greta thought, Why this slow-growing deformity, loss of feeling in the affected part?

The comma fell off her face and off the brother's. The other brother.

Or it had to be traumatically amputated. Like a brother who sticks.

In sex, the sister and brother were one flesh with two heads, two hairdos.

In the bathtub, she reached for his pre-sexual organ. The mother, sad glass, shattered.

The other night, Greta got to be Gregoire, worry that herhis erection would show. S/he wanted the beautiful girl to hold herhim. Touch her thick eyebrows. But that never works.

The part of the nervous system that is the organ of thought. Grete played the piano, Greta played the organ?

The part of the nervous system that is the organ of skin. Its pain, its joy.

First you could read me by touching me. Versus sight-reading.

Nodules from an illness we share. Nervous Cartesian coordinates. But no, she is no dualist!

Musical cells and threads.

The mother, mournful cloth. His face wiped on it?

His = her father's?

The mother used a washcloth to clean the girl's face, but the cloth itself was unwashed, caused bumps or swellings. The skin insistent.

Peripheral nervous system, ephemeral nervous sis tune! Ach Greta, stop it!

The incestuous wordplay could be treated with drugs or with a leper house. But this philosophical anti-system is my nervous system.

In his brain, suicidal pictures. In his central nervous system. The history of the *idea* in philosophy. *Vorstellung* vs. *Darstellung* as representation. She said, Presentation. Nothing prior.

The marks on the skin grew fainter ≠ the marks fainted.

Hysterical yet intelligent. Brainy. Like that Joe or some raven. She could still turn into them!

This paper dirty.

To kill by smashing the skull, like Cain did Abel. Or to hit on the head. Like a nail. They never show the feet, stigmata. Poetical, rhythmical, beautiful.

Gehirn and *Köpfchen* sound better than brain. *Geistesprodukt?*
Geisteskind? The brainchild floated out of her.

She his brainchild: godly papa. She Minerva. Add that Minerva
prose poem here! But I don't move.

Brainstorm and stress not a poetic movement. Or is madness
essential?

Sublimation of madness. Vs. the truly mad ones, who don't create
things.

The brain waves like sound waves or ocean waves. Georg's odd
affinity for water. As a boy of 5, he walked in fully clothed until it
was over his head.

As a girl of 6, Greta walked in and sat down so it was over her head.
Craved to be in over her head or some other motif. Her brother
pulled her up by her hair because big brothers protect little sisters.
When they don't addict them.

Later a phobia of drowning.

They played together in the water, threw sticks, skipped stones, used
kickboards. He could swim well, she couldn't.

I don't remember.

Brain teaser.

The world is all that is the braincase: *Hirnschale, Schädel, Schädelkapsel.*
Georg said *Schädelstätte.*

He said, Stop teasing me. She said, I am not teasing you.

Some brothers brain you for arousing them. Others like it, try to
arouse you back. Or else they started it.

There are many possible brothers.

Threw the stone father so he would skip over the water, not sink.

The mother salt. The brother salt. The father salt.

The meanings shift in all the contexts?

Why is this part numb?

Loss of sensational. Loss of sensual. Of sensation in her extremity.

Influence of Ernst Mach on her brother Ludvik's philosophy? Or reaction again it.

Serious machinery: logic's power.

Loss of empiricist philosophy. Possibilia as nodes in logical space. Tubercular nodules as with Gregor. I have been neglecting him! Turned into a leper. Was consumed by possibility. Paralyzed by three modalities.

Hunger distracted her. Him. Brother, why won't you share your food with me? But he did share it. Only that was later, after she had been starved by the flat, sad mother. Salt. Grete brought food to her deformed brother Gregor, so he wouldn't starve.

Felt.

Felt of the bumper pool table where he beat her, she lost. Was lost? Then they did it against it, not on it like on the regular pool table.

Loss of felt.

*

Trajectory through Others
Took out the thorny redemption book on Trakl, then she didn't read it. Plastic protector like on a puberty sofa. Stays stainless even when making out—although the thighs stick. Don't pull out what pricks

yet, it's good to hurt. The music switched to superficiality, could that save this? Outside, the sky stretched its legs. Homeless white girl under royal blue scaffolding. Two small rectangular cushions, paperback, backpack, broken umbrella. What is it like to be a that? A bag says trash. Beating them up. Queer teen vagrants being beaten. Or older crazies. The mother slapped the pubescent daughter's face because she masturbated to James Kirk, the girl thought, I should run away! Kirk looked sexy with no shirt on, hairless, sweating, wrestling. Lt. Chekhov also sort of hot w/ his accent marks, but in a nerdy, ineptly boyish way, would have to be taught how. In the Bible, the sister liked to dance, was afflicted with leprosy by God because she danced too seductively, proudly aroused Him and her brothers. Or because she was envious of her brother the prophet, proto-messiah, he didn't deserve it! My metaphysics just as impressive! I drink the whole world. It's fizzy, salty. Red Bull for the Minotaur, now Greta or Gregoire. Whereas Victor put on the Planet of the Apes mask, entered the dimmed bedroom in the afternoon while she pretended to be sleeping. Or they dressed up as Batman and Robin, or pirates. The photos were happy childhoods. Grew up not to touch-type, always searching. Sky clenched. Forest sulking. Shapes decide their meanings. Relief to fixate on tattooed wrist bandages, different arc through the labyrinth, sign of a difficult text.

*

Gray Very Light Bluish Notebook
The sky. Clouded over but bright. Almost white, but impure.

My trousers' pale gray leitmotif. I said, I will do the trouser role! Wore male leather shoes size small, autumn leaf brown as per my thesaurus. I named them my Gunters because fighting, warring, struggling. And a girl's pink shirt size large that said Rapid Transit and showed a red Mercury because racing. Stole the shirt from the other Georg in my other book. I.e. from my other self. A girl only has sex in the meaning of a sentence. Meaning in the sex of sentences.

I wish my brother Georg would visit me. I am in my tower or the mental hospital which isn't yet the military hospital, I am hiding from my intended, Ferdl Thurstan. He has bad breath but good manners.

My hair a messy Prince Valiant or The Rolling Stones of *Flowers*, w /
long bangs in my eyes, but not long enough for Georg to scale if I
stick them out through the window.

This is a gray scale: it has eight gray notes. Plus black and white,
the extremes, which strictly aren't gray but rather gray's limits.
Therefore ten notes, which my dictionary says a gray scale typically
has—

The twelve-tone system was something else in radical Viennese
music.

But today is 08.18.11, not .12, and I am 18! Age is vagrant.

Riff more on the numbers, Greta. No! I wanna be free, I'm Davy
Jonesing for it! I do a gray scale that is still chromatic. Include the
accidentals. Also when you feel flat or sharp. The black keys with the
white ones. Black like Davy's straight, thick eyebrows, white like his
large teeth. Anyway, all grays have colors, hues a brilliant one can
see. Pearls can be brilliant, although pearl is gray. Did Davy sing the
lead on *Shades of Gray*, too? Having a Monkee on your back is being
addicted. Her first girlhood album!

Sudden wave of light-headedness. Fear of fainting like a female,
so you have to move quickly to safety. They say nothing serious
is wrong with me, I am being hysterical. I say, I suffer from
labyrinthitis! But they don't yet know what that is. Because I came
too early, precocious, prophetic.

Then I stole away from my brother Georg Trakl, said I am no more
Greta Trakl. Now I hide away from my betrothed Ferdl Thurstan, say
I am not yet Greta Thurstan.

They said organic, he said mechanical, I said either: simply an
instrument. That produces notes, sound. A tune. Via oscillation.

Ball of pitches. Ball of strings. Philosophy a maze to enter.

End of overture.

Temporary blackout, curtains of eyelids fall. Unconsciousness tunes this up.

The I is the truth. But so is the world. I and world as different aspects. Alternation.

The metaphysical key is oscillation. It projects, is the essence.

The form is truth, the content meaning. The matter is language, the motion vibration. The function is to emit, express, sound, resound. Why music is most powerful.

Not something unknowable, not conatus (will to survive), will as ceaseless striving, or will to power (expansion). Rather swinging. Between will and no will, construction and destruction, subjectivity and objectivity, thought and thing, veracity and reality, etc.

The world is everything that will sway. All that oscillates. The set of flips, not fixed things.

Ditto the I. Ergo the truth.

I spied tall, square-shouldered Stig again, in his dark gray wool cap and black t-shirt—but he has a manly mustache and muscles now. Wrong incarnation! Instantly, my Stig-addiction died.

Forget the idea of the sibject, return to the idea of the traject?

I have that idea. I made up the stress, I placed it differently, I invented it!

To traject is to transport, transmit or transpose. To cast or throw over or across.

The middle-aged guy's death rings are not really Wagner's.

False turn, distraction, I as trajection. A point that keeps moving.

So it can rest at mind or body or person or self-consciousness or vibration. It isn't fixed.

If it doesn't brake, don't try to fix it.

The I is not the subject, it includes it. The subject is the human consciousness that can be self-consciousness. But the I is more, does more.

Manuel Kurt's *I think*: here *think* means unify representations? It is active. It is abstract self-consciousness.

Renard Dexter's *I think*: here *think* means hold, believe, have in mind? But isn't it still active? It is individual consciousness.

Ferdl Thurstan's *I think*: here *think* means interpret, and *I* means it, the it that thinks in me. It's the body being active, and the consciousness mistaking itself for thought.

Greta Trakl's *I think*: here *think* means aver. It's active and passive, mind with body, consciousness exposing itself as self-consciousness. But it can split, become its twin and other. Darker, lighter, evil, good. Consciousness can be of one's own alien I. But then is it still an I? Yes, for the I is infinitely divisible—into same and other, stranger, *Fremdling*. Xeno's Paradox!

But must the other be object for a subject, as Ardl would insist? No, because of the sibject. You can be your own brother, sister—even if you are an only child. But then what happens to subjectivity: it's sibjectivity? Or is there subjectivity w/o a subject? Or do I simply need to reconceive of the subject?

My hair smells from being unwashed. It's good that I don't want to talk to Stig now.

The task is to unravel the idea of the swing or swinger. Greta as mood-swinger! Rapid trans it-girl! Also bisexual, thus ready for a good. Therefore a philosopher.

So why do I never get around to that?

The I presupposes the consciousness that can become self-consciousness, and then another consciousness. But the I is embodied: it's a first person that's a trans-I.

I am the truth = the Incarnation. The truth must be incorporated, as says my fiancé, Ferdl Thurstan. The thinking and willing subjects are one: the metaphysical sibject, as say I, Greta Trakl.

Page of yesterday's wrestling: type or tear it up!

*

ÄNGSTLICHER AUGENBLICK/DER TOD UND DAS MÄDCHEN
The door opened, darkness cracked, it scared her, old lady w/ candy bar and box of crayons, coloring in book, foolish smile on her face, phony flowers by Japanese woman, coffee jerkette sickly, Greta, *Bruder*ridden, unable to philosophize, to transfigure to orange color, be irreal, pain replaced by stupor theorem, a drug addict unafraid to swallow, the little girl ate books or what the characters ate in them, such as boys, sucking them off, feasting on them in the maze's center, girl's head on boy's body, bastard of unnatural sex, death and the lass, derivation, unfull stop,

CODA
Dad alas; Dead alas; Dead, a lass; Dead, a loss; Dad a loss; Dad, a less; Did a lass; Did a less; Dead a lust; Dad a lust; Did a lust; Dead a list; Dead a less; Deed a loss; Deed a lust; Deed, alas

INDEFINITE DEPICTION
After Grete, Georg's self-portrait or the other's picture of her punctured or bullet-riddled. Behind her stood her youth with its Exacto knife. It doesn't need to be exact, said Georg, but exacting. *Doch*, retorted Ludvik, erect in military uniform. When they left, alternation metaphysics, altercation poetics. Then solipsism copulates with realism, the I collapsing to unseen obscene point. Of origin of graphic, not novel. Her yellow no halo. Nor vinyl recordings. The shrieking girls who don't belong here, inside me, who screw the cap onto the poem so it can't be drunk anymore.

THE OTHER OCEANIC FEELING
Writing as swimming awkwardly
Not drowning, but
Not getting any closer to land
And feeling suddenly too tired

IF STUCK TO THEIR REALITY
Shivering in black visual rectangle. She tries not to. Hide and Seek,
Catch and Kiss, Truth or Dare. Greta can't create well-formed
formulas. Heidegger on Trakl asinine, don't even speed-read it. Ferdl
sold his books, had beautiful handwriting. Grete's handwriting a
string of OCD double-nooses, 8's, ∞'s sideways. Tall young man's
long fingers with fine, hirsute knuckles. Grete doesn't want him, or
does she want him? I want to be a better person: first, second, third.
Better sister, leitmotif.

THEY SNAP THE SYMBOL STRING
I neglected Gregor, I must bring him some food! All she knows how
to do is to be a girl, music student, sister. Not how to please the
audience: three boys in hipster t-shirts. Will the prose poem/novella
escape the tonic note? Girl shies away from the yawning man.
Towards logic's asymmetrical, ruined face.

BOUND ASSOCIATION
Her transvocals, although a flagrant soprano. Obnoxious nose with
provocative come-hither nostrils. Skeletal, sexual, the girl horrified
the brother, mother, French Lit teacher. Sought or fought the closet
like a Russian antihero. When you're young, the boys like your
boyishness, later they disdain it. Greta made her Ken doll force sex
on her Barbie: cupped hands on abstract breasts and crotch. Also
drew her own superheroes in crayoned G-strings. Why won't my
fiancé fuck me, laments Greta. This meant to be pure sound. Brown
thighs, red t-shirt shouting victory over her semantic a priori, via
synthetic tactics of passion's turning machine. But meaning came all
over her hip bone.

PROXIMITY PSEUDOHAIKU/JAPANESE GRETA
He hung his ink in
My visual field

Spilled over. Huge man
Sniffling compulsively.
Is this my betrothed?

*

VERY SLIGHTLY BLUE GRAY NOTEBOOK
The beautiful part is the part that forms around the irritant: the
version of you that protects you from pain. Hard, lustrous, not soft,
tender, wet. You produce your best self, then become it. Thus you
can exit your sensitive vulnerability, and also the silent brittle shell.

That pearl is worth everything. But you cast yourself to swine. Such
as the literary schemers at the party.

Nobody listened to Wisdom when she roamed the streets,
proclaiming. They said she was non-canonical, apocryphal. Was she
the Holy Spirit/sister? Recursion in the service of the echo. Echolalia
in the device of glossolalia. Speaking in tones.

Could Greta have been healed by Freud? She was a hysteric.
Ludwig's sister Grete went to see Freud, also she assisted him. Being
sick helps you know. Knowing makes you sick. Friedrich's unsister
Lou Salomé also went, accosted, insisted. Was she sick?

I am sick and I know it. Greta knows it.

The Holy Spirit a ghost because she couldn't be seen by most people,
they ignored her. Or because she was dead already, woke up dead,
had died the night before. But her brother Georg saw, he understood.

She was a spirit because they didn't ogle her equivocal body. But
couldn't that be positive? Or because she blurred the letter, went
instead for tone and feeling. A ghost, because she haunted her
childhood haunts, remained a girl, a ghostwriter, or a shadow,
spying on their metaphysics. Little sisters tag along, can be
annoying.

Today my rash came back; the philosophical thoughts formed
ulcerations, disintegrated, started flaking off. I am not beautiful, but

could I be sublime? I could be terrible.

I detest this prose, don't feel anything, decide to practice music and lyrics, attempt some freer *lieder*.

NEIN
She is not ready yet.

*

EXTREMITY / CLOUD
Hospital green = spring green + milk white
forest green + bone white
but before that he lay in the bed
in the mentality
hospital where the other men / soldiers
screamed, hissed, stumbled
cried out for mercy
look, little girl, will you
run away from the father's
degenerate robe or
the guilt-ridden mother
automatons forward, while
the paranoid ladies shriek
insightful interpretations,
this one dirty and misdated, does it matter?
A brother sits on the edge of the bed to play
Hospital with you. Or that game which gives electric
jolts if you don't put the boner in the right
hollow at the base line where a deep
beat cascaded down
the mountain of the apartment building.
That game was called Operations with Variables X, Y, Z.
Something arranged in a series or succession of stages so that
each stage derives from or acts upon the product of the preceding.
Where is my lightning? My cloudland?
Three cloud words of my portable cloud chamber,
or the cloud returned my book
to the library, the hospital was called.
They took the clouds out of my

mouth, took the clouds out of my chest,
the clouds out of my hands.
They did not love my clouds, or me,
they ruin the silence with their social
diseases. Where is my hospital?
It's the other typewriter which is gunmetal
gray. Last night I almost smoked
myself, like Grete Trakl did.
Instead I forced myself to go
to sleep. But at some
point you wake up.

*

MYTH-MAKE-BELIEVING
Haakon as Theseus. Georg in the center. Greta, the ersatz sister, too
impatient to wait outside, brings her piano string and perfect pitch
in with her, follows the big little brother. What shall we do in the
center?

Ball of pitch = world as music.

At the end, my younger brother leaves me on an island called Naxos,
Anxious, XOs, New Yorks, Nexus, Next Us. Then my dark crown of
thorny hair could be transformed by Dionysus/Ferdl Nietzschus into
a gleeful constellation. Consolation? I could fuck all the other boys or
trees, would that bring back Haakon? I fell down on one aria'd knee.
Aria + end = the girl. Very pure/holy or very eager to please. He
stuck his email tongue in my mouth problem, it went too deep, I was
gagging. I thrust him away. Then I missed him. This isn't the right
approach shot, I will be passed at the net, except that doesn't work in
ping pong. Victor taught me, later I taught Haakon. Impatience and
love of thrill brought this forward. Something should be fun. Past
perfect is dead, so strive for imperfection. But this overly aggressive
pitch—

A weird tingling sensation in my left knee, the one that sang before.
Hysterical paralysis at branching path. It's so confusing to be
bitextual.

Wrong machine, where's my masculine pronoun, cried Greta,
disdaining the German neutral, and Georg saw it, felt admiration.
The cock wasted on him, she got the hard-ons. No substance
genitalia, but use is meaning. Ardl felt resentment. So did Greta.
Facing arrows mean logical contradiction or swordplay. Narrative
chest binding. Breast slits unneeded. While the pussy slit is useful for
further pleasure. Gregor anorexic like a girl. Mother a tense anxiety
machine. Georg droned his ego monologue at the old prostitute
as if she were his mama. Ruination of late boyhood. His 5 o'clock
shadow, hers all-hours. Original plumbing. Transman vs. girl with a
dick? Rumination of early girlhood. Junior high fumbled pass, bus
pass, passing out. Words shove together into the subway. I wrote
him because I fell in love with him. Treason's tree sons: they hung off
them, hanged; one did it to himself. Georg witnessed this. Who isn't
partisan? Part a son. The same words ribboned marbles in mouth.
Sourball metaphysics. Exhausted from were-play. Sticky yellowed
flypaper vanitas painting. Back then Greta dressed as one of the
Musketeers, made use of her faint pubescent mustache, clomped in
rain boots, wide leather belt, tan felt hat. Loneliness because no girl
strokes your ersatz, hersatz. Sex idealism: to be is to be perceived:
XX, XY, XZ. XXX = Ex-XX. Magical idealism's new trick. Victor did
magic tricks at kids' parties, things disappeared or changed like
his sister. Georg wrote poems on Novalis aka that Friedrich. Greta
should write poems on Victor aka Vincenzius. Before, free was easy.
Now thick consonants do not help much. Nor do thin gray library
books like that girl's. It's actually a Nietzsche! Ludwig's Grete surely
read him, too, and Ludwig took ideas from him, he read him at the
end of the war. Nietzsche fought his own war. Loneliness because no
girl stroked him as Fritz. Except he hated that name, only his mama
and sister called him that. Lou Salomé said she wanted them to live
as sister and brother, then ran away with Paul Rée whom she didn't
let touch her either. *Her* fault that he was on the fritz! At times this
Friedrich hates her! Also at times hates his sister Elisabeth. Maybe
childhood incest. Maybe AC/DC. See his adolescence, that soused
poet Ernst Ortlip. Back in black! Every association thick like hair or
Friedrich's mustache or a semantic theory. The ascent of philosophy
is a head getting big. He leans into her crawl space. Won't she rub
his ink-stained prick? Straight girls flicker, die out. High def, or

coming down off the acidic trip, trying to theorize subjectivity. Read Herman Hessian as regression in slavery to the ego. Ineluctable connections, ergo no *Mönchin*. Craven forearms, reckless ankles, men high on contraptions, conniptions. Doomed constantly to reread by catastrophic unsureness: Austrian saint or slut?

*

CHILDREN'S BOOK
It's the brother and sister, only reverse it: *she* is Please Gimme, *he* Ax Me No Questions. Papa still Gimme the Ax. Visual disturbance of a man standing before her with an ax. Ambiguity of grinding. Ismael Ax that student mass murderer, Chinese-American with no pure thought experiment. His anger, sorrow, their sorrow, anger. Suicides and mass murders contagious. Decline of culture: Lukerl and Georg felt it, Ferdl wants to resist it, Greta prefers not to think about it. But the universal suffering molests her. Childhood stories get wet when she drops them in the bath.

ESTRANGEMENT
Brutal stranger won't talk to his female companion. Picks at his arm in shame. *He's like killing himself everyday.* Faces made of Silly Putty. Once transferred the comic book panels w/ it. Sorrow over a new dead boy, girl. Trees reprieved unless children.

THERE IS NO GOING BACKWARD
Doch, there is. Deduction of the labyrinth schema.

ORIGAMI BLACKBIRD
Day collapsed its lung. The alien bit her own breast.

SUICIDAL NOTES
Don't know where the loose pages belong. I fit them in here, there. Falsehood of all progression. But how can music escape time? If the notes run away?

PIANOS HAVE HAMMERS
Private labyrinth hammers inside you. Because eternity wants to be let out. Transfigured wallpaper.

ROOM / PRIVATE MAZE
The bedroom walls were hedges. The edges of the bed hedges. The chair was a hedge, the bureau a hedge, the desk a hedge. The t-shirts and pullovers and pants and boots were hedges. The window blinds were actually hedges.

FISSURE KING OF HOLY GRAIL / HOLY GRETL
The father loosed his lance, she left her lenses in. *He* went to Switzerland alone, and another *he* went to Switzerland alone, and *she* should go to Switzerland alone. Which way to the Castle of the Maidens? Seven brothers becoming ravens means Greta would need to add e.g. Stig or Ferdl. New definition of fraternize. Sex better if it's naughty. Why does Ferdl's mouth disgust me? Nihilism versus lists of hits.

6TH GRADE RANKINGS (AGE 12)

Sexy:	Smart:	Funny:	Handsome:	Sweet:	Charming:
Antoine	Ludvik	Victor	Antoine	Gregor	Antoine
Georg	Gregor	Gregor	Haakon	Antoine	Victor
Haakon	Georg	Haakon	Georg	Victor	Haakon
Victor	Haakon	Antoine	Victor	Georg	Georg
Gregor	Victor	Georg	Ludvik	Haakon	Gregor
Ludvik	Antoine	Ludvik	Gregor	Ludvik	Ludvik

Make-Out:	Dance:	Good Body:	Talented:	Knightly:
Antoine	Antoine	Georg	Georg	Antoine
Georg	Georg	Antoine	Gregor	Georg
Haakon	Victor	Haakon	Ludvik	Gregor
Gregor	Haakon	Ludvik	Victor	Victor
Victor	Ludvik	Victor	Haakon	Haakon
Ludvik	Gregor	Gregor	Antoine	Ludvik

*

TRUTH OR *LIEDER* / 12 WORDS OR LESS x 12
Thin wrist apology
Incest semantics
Or crumpled yellow
V-nicked sister
Floated notes

We scratched the accent
Big Chinese truth tree
Leafing now
Leaving

Impressionable
Metaphysical
Pigeon
Boxing
God said
Claymation
's a lot of work

Yellow notebook
Shout in hair!
2-D fear
Try out
Canary

Thought balloon said, Ach!
Yellow world backed off
Power chord riffs
Rifts

Blue world balled
Detached sis
Trail of pearls
Parole of petals

Hit the flick
Of brother paper
Painful prefix
Liquid sister
Flip-out book

No sound
Unsound
Sound proof

Soundproof
Sound off
Soundless poof

Ishmael took two hits
Of Ishmael / Greta
Dots of youthtruth
Spin-art /
Spirograph

Georg's flickerbook
Dark slow
Movement
Sixteenth pain note
Teen signature
Does Grete

Tilted wood labyrinth
Royal blue marble
Brother won
Hyper fingers
Also Etch A Sketch

Yesterday's fluorescence
Madly shaking legs
Epileptic
Minus Feodor's ecstatic
Metaphysic
Love test

X
If they were ludes, they'd make you want everyone. Unquiet
interludes. But also make your hand numb. Is it too late for Greta to
try Ecstasy? That band X had male and female lead vocals—lovers
but not siblings. Still!

THE SIBLINGS GRIM: SISTER AND BROTHER / S
The Siblings Glam, Glum, Graphic. The Siblings Grime, Groan. The
Siblings Gone.

ILLEGITIMATE ALLUSIONS
Heights of the brother Haakon. Wiry hair, wire-rimmed spectacles.
Huge hoodie. Strong bejeaned thighs. The weight of the brother
when he lies on you, his sad, weird, gentle, playful tongue behind
his teeth behind his lips. Clean-shaven visage presses your chest
down so you can hardly breath. The drama of the true scenario
an invisible hair shirt. Cloud book cover. White, no photo. Back of
letters, head. But in the dirt, like one who plants the corpses as/or
flowers.

When Greta went to Berlin, first she stayed with Ludvik while Georg
wandered. Then she moved to Ferdinand, where Georg visited.
Haakon moved into the room of Georg. Then Ludvik went off to
war. Haakon moved into the room of Ludvik. Then Georg went off
to war. Greta lived in the same room with Georg in Vienna, but that
was when they were teenagers. Greta never lived in the same room
with Haakon. If she did, would she have slept with him? Or had
insomnia with him? Greta never went off to war. But Greta went off.
Like a gun or a wanderer. A bomb. An angry person. An alarm.

ALL THE INTERCONNECTIONS
What is incest, in its essence?

Incest is not essential, it is a family resemblance concept. As with
Greta.

Incestuous relations w/ Ludvik via grandiosity, indominability,
thoughts, philosophy.
Incestuous relations w/ Gregor via passivity, spirituality, tones,
fantasies.
Incestuous relations w/ Victor via obsessiveness, excitability, moods,
memories.
Incestuous relations w/ Haakon via melancholia, sensitivity,
fascinations, repetitions.
Incestuous relations w/ Georg via morbidity, intensity, compulsions,
madnesses.
Incestuous relations w/ Antoine via loneliness, impulsivity, spirits,
longings.

Cf. actual Grete w/ her Georg. And their five siblings—but no, they weren't close to them, only to each other. Like orphaned twins. So keep the others out of this book.

The shift from *e* to *a* in *Greta* is from second to first avowal, person. Or from energy to agony. The sense of *his* future blowing toward you from the past. The wish to be covered in yellow. Not of petals. She lives me, she lives me not.

It hurts if the ghost walks beside you, his long arm slung around your girlish shoulders. But this time, you don't stiffen, pull away.

*

THICK GRAY UNNOTEBOOK (ANOTHER MAZE, OR TWO)
I went otherworldly, got lost in a new ancient version: rather than Georg or myself as the Minotaur, Ferdl as him, and I played the hero. Søren was Daedelus/Sylvanus, who'd designed the maze, and my very holy brother Georg/Geordie waited for me outside it. Had given me lines of text to follow back out, and pitch-blackness to gag Ferdl's mouth. Then the Austrian doctor, serious proposition, said, Tell me your *true* family history. Only he couldn't help me, since my incessant alternatives made him sleepy like Veronal. I ran away.

Our tutor Feodor used to read us stories of incarceration, they came from his huge brow and wild St. Petersburg beard, and they showed how there might be some good in imprisonment, even for the innocent. But *our* house of the dead scared me. Softly Greta asked Georg, What do you think?

*

ANTI-ANXIETY DRUG BUST
I won't be able to decipher this   handwriting later, because it won't   be mine anymore.
The cold and the   stimulants. Snorting ice crystals. Two of my brothers whispered   crystallized. Crystal meth i.e. discursive
        purity. Beautiful form or   this blows.
If I move to their meaning table, will the world   blow up?
I lost my   preferences, somebody stole them. Who   am

I?   Scared of choking on my own   saliva. Muttering into a
personal logical   device. Can I just—? I don't want   to
but—   Yeah yeah. Low murmur of constant connection.   I
don't want   to be   connected!
Skateboarder as rough trade. Ludvik liked   friction. Greta
couldn't   ice skate.
The anti-anxiety drugs won't work because they're not the
                        truth or different   musics.
The mystery of when   it disappears. How it can be taken from you
all at   once.
To live w/ the pain, yes. But also to live w/   the anxiety.
The machinery is   out to get me! Georg?   Geordie
It was better when they kept   the machine away from her, so she
wouldn't plug herself in,   overcharge herself.
Twin batteries, yellow   brother and sister, tomorrow's performance-
anxiety   curfew.
Soothing, phlegmatic? That's a Sucret, menthol. Or   secret
Ludens.   Playing with   yourself.
Two   tall boys w/ beaky noses, wavy dark hair, narrow
faces, small eyes, rebelliously wispy mustaches. *I just might   get
some   sleep tonight.* No I won't, for I will be watchful   Gregoire.
Stop rubbing   your eyes, all the lashes are falling out!
Louis Braille gave himself an infection by rubbing his eyes
with the   all. The children's book showed it. He invented a
language of pimples, it was teen, like   feeling trapped
inside an Edvard Munch painting. I cannot stay   here. If it's
intolerable, poke out your eyes w/ paper   clips. The girl's
mouth bites the brother's   back.
The song played again, it was the same although   nobody
noticed. Georg is insanely   repetitive.
Impure forms of intuition and concepts of understanding.   Or
          misunderstanding.
The betrothed's book is violet, white, yellow. It is   portable.
The ones who taste, hear colors. Greta reads tastes, sees   everything
turned into   writing.   Eats books.
The concept of taste or art is a judgment calling of   mouth
wash. Speech or the sweet & sour   new life. In the mouth,
flowers of taste   buds. Idea of girlishly budding talent. The
German   Romantics' fantasy about teleology of nature.

Ferdl Thurstan knows the truth, throws stones at   glosses,
hearses. Lip   gloss for girls vs. glossaries, glass how-to's. One
sibling sees   more, another buds.   Mirror theories of
meaning or appearances, things in the mirror are closer   once
they've disappeared. Nothing stays   far enough   away. Will
you visit me in the   insane asylum, dearest brother? Will I
          recognize you?
This was supposed to halt two ideas ago. Definitely   desperate.
Historical, eccentric and progressive: that third,   romantic
Friedrich's orbit. I could call him   Holden, whose brother died
and who   loves his little sister. Clutch her in the rue. Catch her
in the why. Like my   papa, who took me for walks by
abysses, cliff-hangers. Cliff dwellers only need apply.   The I.V.
league. Lying there in   hysterical paralysis, Grete as his fiancée
prophesies the end   of Ferdl. Steals his thunder. Thought
of passive   Gregor. Fear of syphilis. Sylvanus made the
labyrinth. Greta   seems already to be thrown   into it like a
fit or   glittering Superball or pink Spaldeen.   Every seven days
another youth falls   prey to Ferdl Thurstan, who eats him. One's
talking with Marcus, he is a good mensch named   Geoff, he
admires my books and languages. I am   unfit for duty,
amoral, conceptually   herniated. Billy the sailor still comes here,
do I have to fuck him also?   I am so tired. A *tractatus* threads my
eyes. Slowly, the   dread retracts. ReTrakls.

*

Thin Gray Notebook
This isn't high up, it's off to the side. Real life's rib cage.

The gray went from dark to light and back. I cried, No equilibrium!

Ferdek just another master/philosopher. He cried, Self-mastery!
Stroked his cowboy mustache. Wrangled decadence.

The alternation is between pain and thralldom. In the exact center
lies the void, it's why you have to keep moving. Boredom =
emptiness.

Grete's mama Maria was merely a depressive, she wasn't ever an exuberant mother like Greta's mama Marya could be, every so often.

The view *sub specie aeternitatis* is not from above, it's from the side. On the same level but further off. Thus near to something else.

My brother and I loved the distance, it was our secret nearness.

I smell rotting garbage from the garden. Because I am not high enough.

I want to get high, but my body can't take it anymore. Grete's body more fragile than Georg's, mine so precocious it's almost dead already—

No future is punk, no wave is past! The no's important. The idea of the continual yes is a vapid idea. Yes dies into no, no revives as yes. Like chance contortions, Mars bars of music, teenage Jesus and the jerking off, our DNA, no-yes New York—how they come back! If you let them.

The males are control freaks. Even Ferdek.

But I get tired of my girlish breasts so I take them off, have a boy's smooth chest, write this notebook w/ my shirt off. Or I have a notebook for a chest, write these boys titless.

All the motifs Ferdek and I shared made us fall in love. Then I said, Let us act like brother and sister. Do not touch me. Of course that was disingenuousness.

The problem of suffering is the only problem. It shouldn't be called evil.

It doesn't matter if this is bad. It is still beautiful.

It will be brilliant because I am a genius! Only shy at parties, with small talk.

At the outer world the music was wet.

I think now that the Scandinavian girl will love me.

The boys such as Ferdek and Gregor are queer girls hopelessly loving straight girls.

Like tomboys loving straight men.

It's raining men iff *it's raining men* is true.

Sex is what will ruin your philosophy.

Not sex: lack of sex! Sexual frustration. Or just: sexuality?

That's not true: it gets transfigured into your sentences.

Intensity of desire = intensity of metaphysics.

Further, there's the philosophy of sex, including incest metaphysics, incest semantics, incest of metaphysics and semantics, how they touch each other's privacy. Why do I only touch on this topic, tease it, why don't I fuck it?

It's raining meanings iff etc.

I want to lock my door but the lock is broken. The prophet is supposed to come to fix it. Or the mountain.

Out there was too peopled. The other projects sat close and talked in distracting voices. Their hair dirty. Once a Swiss girl named *die Lulu* cut off Samson's flirty hair. It fell into another novel. Gregor Samsa→Gregoire/Ishmael via the Samuel/Shemuel inference rule. The arrow Ishmael's symbol when it isn't logical, conditional. The G shows Gregor staring down in consternation at his harder-on, which only points back at himself. W/ Gregoire, it's a pure dildo: how the idea *feels*. I think I already wrote that. Repetition-compulsion like a military habit w/ training in mystery. Self-mystery, not self-mastery! Repeat the word until it turns into bare sound.

Greta also liked uniforms. She wore a tie. Then Wladek ran away. He felt threatened. I had an affair with him, now he acts like it never happened.

It hurts to be alone.

My voice was like Ferdek's but I did not know it yet. He tutored my brother. I was busy studying with Fedka. No, I was busy lolling around with Gregor.

Gregor.

It has to be Gregor. A pale gray bluish octavo notebook. Because philosophy is too strenuous, and I feel sickly, so I get high on parables, aphorisms. I mean drunk. Under the influences.

APHORISMS VS. PAROXYSMS
Is it also why, as a maiden, I fell in love with Ferdl? *Wie Schade, dass es nicht hielt. Aber kein Mitleid!* Now we're finally married.

PALE GRAY BLUISH OCTAVO NOTEBOOK
Do my words not sound like Gregor's because I am a bad person? Or is there a notebook like a door waiting for me to open it and enter, then it would save me? If I, Greta, perish here, will I, Gregoire, come alive inside another, future book?

BOOKISH
Buch, ich. BookIshmael. Bookish male. Equals girl!

*

THEORY OF SYNONYMY (INCEST COLOR THEORY)
Gray = black

THEORY OF SYNONYMY #2
Georg = Greta

THEORY OF SYNONYMY #3
Lurid = ill lit

Love
In the thesaurus left by their father, they lay in the same paragraph of darkness, separated only by a comma. But even that was too much, so they broke the syntactic rule. Did it in poetry.

Narcissus
In one version of the myth, as he gazed into the pool, he saw his sister's reflection staring up at him.

In one version of the fairy tale, as she stared into the writing, she heard her brother's inflection singing up at her.

Truth
Instead of my brother Victor pulling me out of the water, my brother Georg pulling me in. Male siren.

Not Jesus
First the stone skips over the surface of the water, then it sinks. Did Georg ever skip? Brother and sister skipped class, lay in the playroom. Let he who is without sin cast the first us.

Family Dissemblance
You sound like your older brother, your younger brother sounds like you. Then the poem skips, repeats, you're exposed. Here is a hand, with its fingers in the other's mouth, touching their tongue.

The way the secret sends you to an alternative world, a twins' world where all is possible: a set of sentences. A paracosm.

Dream's Undone Night Tongue / Traum und Umnachtung: Impure Homo Trans of Pt. 1
On evening/ward, zoom in on Greta's her fading/father; in darkling room/stammer fears her stoner armpits/eyelids of mother and off dank boy/knobs lost/wasted the fucked/flesh of anarchic/one tender/dare tart girl sex. Manchild/malaise erring into/erratic he/her sick sign of cunthood/kidhood, air filled fun/foam/with/of crank height/sickness, shrieks and sinister/darkness, silenced game in stony garden, odor that he drew rats/tits/fit her into twilight/damning the hope/off. Entered us/lust blue mirror treat/tract the slimmer figure/

Gestalt/Gretal tore sister/sibling, and he plunged/staggered as dead into dark ill. Nights broke his mouth like a red/rotten fruit aagh and the stars glazed/glinted over his speechless/truer/horror/grief. His dreams felt up/fulfilled the altered house of father. At evening he went gamely over the fear fallen/abandoned freed of/graveyard, or he saw louche/losers/corpses in the demanding dead room/taught in chamber, the green flecks of decomposing/their wasting of heir/hair in beautiful/shining hands. At the fortress/cloister her brother begged for a hunk/stick of bro/bread; the shadow of a black horse/gripping/rape scene sprang from the ink/dark and shocked him. When he lagged in his cool bed, unspeakable tears overcame him. But it was no one, who had put a hand upon his forehead. When fall/despair/her hips came, he went/kinky/goner/gangly/ganged her, a hell-seer/clairvoyant, in brown-eyed awe. Oh, the hours/standing wild rapture/her dicking, the upended/evening him/I'm groaning loose/flesh, yeah-yeah-saying/young/yoked them/jagged. Oh, the soul, the lights-out/lies' *lieder* yellowed whore/roars sang; fiery high fidelity. Still he saw long/longing in the star-eyes of her standard logic problem Greta's/Cretan, feeling with shuddering hands the coolness of the altar stones and bespoke/spat out the heirs' worthy saga of blue quelling. Oh, the silver fashions/falsehoods/falsies and the fuck/fruits, that from crumpled trees/boymen fell. The accord of his steps filled him with pride and contempt for mankind/everyone. On the way home *trayf* he found an abandoned stronghold. Fallen gods stood in the garden, grieving her hint-reading/him-training in evening. But it seemed/shone to him: here I lived forgotten years. An organ chorale filled him with God's shiver. Uppers in darker hollow he broke herhis sign of tags/days, locked and stole and hid/fear-blocked himself/sick, a flaming/*flame on!* wolf/whiff, before the white unface of the mother. Oh, the hours/seconds when he/she sank down with stoned mouth in the starry garden, the shadow/shitting/shattered/shudders this murder's overcoming him. With purple forehead he went into the more and God's torn/ire chastised his metal shoulders; the birches/barking I am storm, that's darker Greta, that signed made his benighted fatal/father/paths. Hate burned his heart's/hearse, whole/vile lust, do her as he did/violated the silent kid in the green/groaning summer garden, in whose radiance sigh I am naked anguish he knew/recognized/concocted his night-darkened/deranged countenancing/I am face. Wait, evening happens on the window/face her, while from purple flowers a gray corpse/groping/ rib cage/Greta/girl ripper, dare/her tit/twat/tried dead/death. Oh, you/her towers/tremors/torments and glocks/bells/clocking; and the shadows of night fell stonily/like stones on off them./Stoning them.

UNTITLED
I feel scared.

*

MENTAL HEMOPHILIA
With poverty approaching, Greta took sick and hemorrhaged possibilities. Youth bruised easily. Sister and brother, hypersensitive, used to stay home from school. He memorized colors, she taught herself musics.

CHROMATISM, SERIALISM
My twelve-tone technique demands twelve moods per paragraph. What if you could put twelve moods into just twelve words? Does a word have a mood outside the context of a sentence? Could it, with a phrasing? Phrasing's musical. Do a philosophy of phrases. As of phases: my oscillation/vibration metaphysics. It's not a system.

THEORY OF HETERONYMY (PUT TWELVE MOODS INTO JUST ONE WORD?)
Gray = ash gray, crystal gray, dove gray, field gray, French gray, gunmetal gray, iron gray, lead gray, pearl gray, silver gray, smoke gray, stone gray

TWELVE-WORD POEMS/SECOND VIENNESE SCHOOL GIRL, PT. 1
Put bilingual verses here: five *Lieder* for *fünf Brüder*. But I can't, something's wrong.

*

METAPHYSICS OF FEELINGS
It isn't true until it's in words.
        The rectangular blackness hurt her shoulders.
Haakon loved and admired Georg and collected the eyelashes he dropped. My manly eyebrows are falling off because I masturbate too much.

Some brother left and buried his tongue under a tree in the park, but the park is enormous, and Greta didn't know which tree to embrace, rub herself against.

The metaphysics of feelings such as black jacket. Or book jacket. Thicket. How I am hacking through it. Briar Rose and the prince at once. Getting scratched.

Tomorrow has to leave. Does it matter?

The view *sub specie aeternitatis* is supposed to show the beauty, artistry. But I never dream that I am flying anymore.

The world as feeling. He said raw feels. She isn't sure she liked it.

Do not read the proofs or newspapers! Black and white versus gray. Too overt.

Melancholy slows the key frames. Notes or objects.

Her words are smarter than she is. Therefore this is a prophet.

Though it isn't true until it's wordless?

FITS PERFECTLY

Greta couldn't walk right, the ground uneven, shifting. Is it because her hair's too long and straight now? The tall, noble brother Haakon turned his face sideways, offered encouragement. Then he went away. He is always going away. Words grow faint. The other language doesn't answer your eyebrows. Having nothing in common with yourself, *a fortiori* the others. My brother Gregor said that. There is no rule, but there is unruliness. No ground, but there is groundlessness: girl's size M.

ABANDONMENT

Greta, alone among the boys, dies down. Denotes.

CONFESSION #4

Having the dangerous stuff here, and swallowing it all alone, and waiting for the world to change. That means yourself.

TRANSCENDENCE VS. IMMANENCE

If self-consciousness is not the ground, and God is a lie, then what? Gutter, abyss? When the street is a book.

EITHER WHAT'S BELOW OR WHAT'S ABOVE

Ferdek announced, The unconscious instincts or self-overcoming. I cried, *Das ist super* or subliminal!

TIMELY OBSERVATION
My super's name is Bolek; he hates everyone. Reeks of
Übelmenschlichkeit. Ganz üblich. Lately, he quit dying his hair.

SWINGER
Greta's tongue could play tart in either sense.

VISION
The abject person hidden under the blanket, only tortured feet with
sores on the soles protruding. Greta walks by him, looks away.

ANOTHER CONTRAST
He sleeps, Greta suffers insomnia.

LITTLE SISTER
I cannot reach the height of my brother.

INSIGHT
From that scene in the movie, coming to realize that a gun would be
the best way after all. Like Greta.

ETYMOLOGY
When did *come* come to mean come?

ISMS
Realism, idealism, solipsism, extremism, expressionism, irrealism,
unrealism, cynicism, witticism, perspectivism, prism, cataclism (sic),
subjectivism, objectivism, romanticism, emotivism, milksoppism,
masochism, jism, eroticism.

GRETELOGISMS
First personalism, sisterism, ink milk splinterism.

NO ENVY
The brothers got the milk. But Greta preferred Nestlé Quik.

EXPOSURE
Actually there was no milk. The brothers got the face, Greta

preferred the blond hair of the nanny. Whereas Grete alone was nursed by the mama. Never mind that.

NO ENVY #2
The brothers got the spunk. Greta preferred her fantastic spiritual prick.

EXPOSURE #2
It was long, thin, pale and teenage, sensitive but able to rise to the occasional music.

EXPOSURE #3
A word in her hand is worth two in the bush! Greta as bi-sexed and bisexual! Her pussy insists: I *can* have the All. For licks, it gives some lip.

NO ENVY #3
Spirit ≠ letter. Ludvik did the ladder, Greta did the spit.

CHASTISEMENT (THOUGH NOT S/M)
You are supposed to be reading and writing about Søren/Sylvanus on God now. *The Instep of Irony.* How the shag rug gets pulled out from under you. It, too, was just a covering over the abyss.

FACE A DIFFERENT DIRECTION, MAYBE WALK BACK TO WHERE SHE WAS A NOTEBOOK
But the idea of the maze is not the Absolute. The Absolute might or might not make it into this story.

PERTINENT PARADOXES
The Isolate Paradox, the Dissolute Paradox, the Resolute Paradox, the Desolate Paradox, the Insolent Paradox.

PURITY IS TO WILL ONE GROOVE THING
Haakon said the idea of rain in the room is too much, Greta said Edvard Munch had snow in his room. Cf. the wardrobe in the first book of Narnia, also referenced in the pubescent poem when she, as Mina, first exposed herself. No new ideas because her forms are eternal. But none of her loves are Platonic, nor even Neo-Platonic.

Although sometimes she attended a Plotinus class.

Always Too Hot or Too Cold
Haakon and I, Greta, pulled our shirts off, then put them back on, then took them off again in iteration. Meanwhile we plotted thefts of Wagner.

Role-Play Poetics
Haakon collated Georg while Greta fellated him. Haakon atomized him while Greta sodomized him. Haakon listened to him and spoke with him, Greta molested him and spanked him. Haakon played ping pong with him, Greta played with herself on top of him. Haakon dirtily translated him, Greta filthily translit him. Haakon dreamily read him, Greta speedily dreamed him. Of course, sometimes they switched roles.

Incest Poetics' Ethics
Am I still a good sister, person, *Mensch*, if I make out and off with my brother's writing? It's so aggressive. But that's how Georg likes me. Also, he knows there's more to me. He lets me be gentle, fragile, quiet, melancholy too. Sometimes he tops me. We come in each other with black ink, score with each other, switch who's the girl, who's the boy. Are loud or silent. Our sweat is silver, sour, shameless.

Greta, Longing
Georg, ich vermisse dich, with your sorrowful spirit, detachment, passivity, sharp scents, rough hair, bitter skin, sweet spit, intoxicated creativity, isolation, asceticism, self-accusation, infinite interiority. *Liebster Bruder,* I want to leap into you again, be your she-knight of faith. Ritalin's *Ritterin!*

*

Bivocals / Snorting Parataxis
Phraser set to stunned. Existentialism took the form of Georg or *Star Trek.* Kirk strutted in his nylon ochre shirt, *Georg schrieb über Sterne.* I flunked astronomy, still I look. Celestial objects vs. subjects. Rooftop screamings. Stars bolted into the dark blue as piercings. *Dieser Traum* about falling backwards over the roof railing. Sorrow of no insurance. The forms can't be filled out like a pubescent girl's

chest. Fedka another tutor, Søren not. Make him the neighbor who clomps now. This narrative ravenous and *vergesslich*. Greta snacked on boys' backs in tenniswear at camp. Not yet their Snack Package Instant Hard-Ons. Victor's better racket. First they stuck together, people thought they were freakish. Greta didn't shower, got crushes on unisex instructors. Victor disappeared into his own video game or striped terrycloth headband. Greta flung her racket when she lost, was a sore loser. Victor grinned sheepishly when he won. They watched *The Twilight Zone*, giggled together. No, that was back home, before. Don't watch TV in the afternoon unless you are a sick schoolchild. The paragraph could slant upward so the empty page would become a snowy mountain. Trying for the edge *zwischen Leben und Tod*, ecstasy and self-destruction, rapture and despair, *hier und dort*, male and female, reason and unreason, *Konzept und Intuition*. To get away from the family state of affairs. *I've gotta get out of this place, 'cause I'm 18, I get confused every day, I'm 18, I don't know what to say, I'm 18 and I like it,* sings Greta, drunk in the Häagen-Dazs store. Sneaks a cigarette. But that other girl, also drunk, high on the ledge to shoot a photo of the *Nacht*-sky when she tumbled. Teen angst, loneliness, wildness, reckless impulses. No poetic words to break her fall, which she alone experienced. I feel sick at the thought of her. Then the witnesses. The losses are uncut, strangely arousing. Is someone sitting here? *Nein, aber etwas ist.*

INVOLUNTARY POVERTY
Grete's friends couldn't always help her. She inhaled their money after using Georg's, which was originally Ludwig's. Once divorced, her ex-husband browbeat her for cash, while she became unemployable. Must I be a servant? She did drugs, had tantrums. The Breaking Sanatorium of the Sister of His Cross and the Mannish Neurological Institute of New Freedom couldn't cure her of curare. The picture didn't change, had too many red, white, yellow, black and blue peaks and valleys. Smooth thighs of a teen girl cross the visual field of Gregoire, who hurts. Being Greta helps?

ACCENTUATION
Polish music like Chopin, Russian music like Tchaikovsky. A stranger flipped through used scores. Greta wasn't composing.

MUSICAL CRIB SHEET
Now it's gone. How can you ever say why?

WELTSCHMERZ

My brother Victor is still short, slender, half-Asian, with cropped
dark hair, a thin mustache, small eyes, bad skin, refined extremities,
cool pants, skinny kicks, female friends. He is my elder brother,
but he looks younger. We're almost the same size. He's tender and
eager to please. He talks a lot. He could be Greta as a transman, if
she weren't playing Georg's double. And if his friends were *Männer*.
But I'd prefer to be a Chinese brushstroke on a Song dynasty monk's
landscape painting—which is also a poem and a philosophy. A
dream.

HOME SCHOOLING VS. DAY SCHOOL

Hollow, she wore the mask of her dead brother Georg, lifted from
Haakon, who lifted it from Davyd Wojnarowicz when Trakl read /
was Rimbaud. Except she didn't always wear it, sometimes she
practiced kissing on it. Before, she'd worn the mask of Gregor lifted
from herself when Gregor was still Kafka, wishing to lay his Jewish
head in a Czech girl's lap. Too much spit in your mouth suggests
excessive cogitations. The Jesus postcard slipped, it was tired of
carrying him in his red robe. I am tired of carrying my brother
unless my father. Nailed to him for the longest sex scene in cosmic
history. The suicides besides Jesus go to hell or get buried in outcast
graveyards just with family. But she whispered to Georg because
she was inside his face. His mouth. Or they were close like the two
12 year-olds in that Swedish vampire movie *Let the Right One In*.
Ludvik can't keep up because he's too reasonable. Until he's musical.
Being mad is less a poetic motif than an ecstatic motive. Only, now
it's going the other way, the nervous breakdown turning her to
stone. In the Narnia book, fondling each other in the wardrobe. I saw
four of my brothers yesterday, so I am info. Gregoire's love-interest
was in Scandinavian, while Greta wanted her sister-in-law Lola to
let her in too, like that '70s John Travolta single, they could practice
their vampiric kissing on each other, be ready for the boys. Blood on
Greta's mouth and chin. If you bite the book, it doesn't die, it lives
forever. Does the father live forever, does his son? Greta doesn't want
to live on after them. But the world bell rings for translation class.

*

DIRTY TRANSLITIONS
Tried to write my *Elektras* with Sophocles' tragedy making out
with Georg's *Elis* versions, but Georg rubbed too hard, imposed
his rhythm, so I could not compose myself. Daughter would wax
melancholic not mournful, project survivor-guilt onto mother, crave
absent brother—since Elektra and Orestes/Oskar also arguably had
a thing.

SUBBED TITLES
To The Girlboy Elektra (*Only Version*), On the Youth Elektra (*Second
Fusion*), Elektra (*Drastic Vision*), Elektra (*Dirty Versing*), Elektra
(*Dreaded Verso*)

*

ES IST
It is warm and your back gets exposed. Religious music. A total
stranger touched my book with his unclean hands. It was as if he
touched my waist. Or my beloved fragile brother's. I must protect
him, although he is the older one. I cried out, Leggo my Georg! But
only on the inside. On the outside, she frowned like an ungenerous,
unfrightened girl. Then smiled like a polite one, sought forgiveness.
The stranger was sick with tuberculosis or some other highly
contagious lung disease.

Es sind no angels, they died in the brother's poetry. Only angles and
ungirls.

*

DESPERATION
Inexpressible. Why not do it today, 12.02.11? Because you don't have
the unglue gun?

Earlier, the sky a silver-white light and blue slate Dutch painting,
now pale orange baby aspirin. The book a green dead man. His
rotting lips. Hair that kept growing, not because he was a rocker.

Tired of grief that keeps growing. Why can't I play cock rock
anymore?

Greta's 28, how old is Gregoire? Say 38, so ending in 8, infinity erect.
Therefore not infinity anymore. Brother and sister played Crazy
Eights. Ate craziness. Adam and Eve. Start a new tradition: neither
spring nor fall? Winter. In January Ferdl came back to life, Gretl goes
forward to death? St. Januarius, bisexed martryred patron saint of
androgyny, with periodic bleeding. Nimbus around my head a halo
or else a rain cloud = thunderhead, ergo Ferdl Thurstan. Should I,
Greta, resubmit myself to my husband's awkward pawing? His left
hand hesitant and polite, right hand grasping and brutish. And that
ridiculous pubic hair mustache. But I deserted him months ago, and
there is no going back.

Liquefaction of blood, never inserted a tampon into a notebook.
Greta! They howl on the rock 'n' roll record. A party she doesn't
want to laugh at. Radiant light turning the buildings black. *In fact
there is no correlation between the temperature and the variable speed of
the liquefaction, but there is variation in weight and in the apparent bulk of
the blood in the glass phial.* Sometimes it/she behaves unpredictably.
That singer Davvid had a nervous breakdown, quit testifying, took
a blood bath. Greta's clothbound books used to bleed red when she
bathed, read—

The next page missing.

If I made it to January—

I will not make it to January.

The typing faint, fragile. The handwriting small yet bold, messy.

I miss the subsequent sheet of paper. It contained *An Ishmael In
Dream*, my cover version of Georg's *Sebastian im Traum*. Redo it as
Georgchen I'm Dream?

No, please do something else. It woke up.

*

DEATH BY MASTURBATION
Doing yourself...in. Greta's gallows humor. Some men hang
themselves to increase their pleasure. Otherwise, more nooses go on
women, girls. (See the *Thieves Trilogy*.)

*

ALIEN—ANTIGONE VERSES

Characters:	*Plot:*
Antigone—Antigone—Greta	Not exactly like the original.

Oedipus—Anton / Antonius—Antoine
Jocasta—Mashenka—Marya
Teiresias—Moira / the Sis—Marlene
Ismene—Grigori—Gregor
Polyneices—Georgi—Georg
Eteocles—Lyudovik—Ludvik
Kreon—Ferdin (Victorino's tutor)—Ferdek
Euridice—Victorino—Victor
Theseus—Feodorus (Antigone's former tutor)—Feodor
Haimon—Haamon—Haakon
Chorus / Furies—Girls
Chorus Leader—Lolya—Lola
Priest / Stranger / Sentry-Messenger—Greagoir—Gregoire
Laios—Lars—Laurence

1 Wrecks

Ice-stunned   stoned on   unguessed   the guestGeist
         hits.
It's ash   schönshame   Anton-sign   zu   a kin.
Undone gold, hellbent gelben fear Mauermourning doubts   the
         Sis's   hint.
Lies ring city steps. Glass storming. Doch dark   black rumor
         lepersleep er   schläft.
Her-son of pain, I am   gray mirror.

Abendt by Ferdin's / Moira's / Mashenka's t,old, we d,rank unselves,
         cried bro,ws.
Rotting s,licks   glühtgluts the f,earsome,   leaves   black,out of
Tendergentlesanftesofter sonata, frohfröliches lookinglaughing.

Beautiful schonshown as stillest,ill   silence   of   Nachtnothing
Of dark,er   plan:
Move on with harder tones, now   hurtknown stars, whiteheat
        starstern.

When Lars, corpse   ge,worden,   lasts ist
Nixzeit showszeigt itsich clearly   in my city   hainsight
We wander   beingshattered   rotten   Moira hanged,
        Mother   hid
Und our woundround eyes follow her mad   f,light to brooches.
Amended Anton sinks into vice's earsores   pools,   en g,raves
        yearning.

In cold killclouds bared, fate branches yellow, goes two-gunned
        future hym n.
In clean   hands, Lolya trägt die   ending: Bro und Wein en.
And riferiffed w/ on voided freedom, Anton singt to girl of
        Kammerclamor

With its   ernst-inscri   bed   Antlitz angle. Dares   torn
        Tote,d,aughter:
Touch me, don't fear.   Ge,wrecked   girl   I watch nothing.

2 @Clone Place (Copse)

Silent is the   devastation's garden   vag,rant doubles enter,
W,here young   naivete   of furious girls' tunes   tells.
H,is breath ,   ordeal's black _{ice,}   er satz, s,he drinks s,he.

Hands raise alterity of blue   once_{-was,}   lack   or
Order of cold nigh,t   with white   arms of _{Twilight Next Gen brother,} sister.

Lolya's harmonic w/ gang, while Antigone *his* wreck-room's
        interred signer is,
Where   loneliness   lasts, and rash intoxication of _{long-ago} Anton,
Whom   the nosy chorus-girls dread. Note his dras,tic   singing.

Already is Antigone manned and appearing in   dark   ling _{o}   ,

While he   astounds, arms and legs   moves,
Inviolate or   violet $_{\text{hell}}$ purports. Grigori sidles in to them tell:

In wrestling lose themselves dual estranged br,others, black
        November destruction
Of you $_{\text{our branch}}$ ignore they, and Ferdin would Antonius near out $_{\text{leper}}$
    wall.
Before were   the high/low br,others or at least Georgi   saintly, now
Both sink both into sightlessness, sound $_{\text{ungentle}}$ with war's sense less
    $_{\text{mad}}$ ness.

How alone we are we   de,clares An,ton, with my   winding   to end
In dying that despair's $_{\text{dark}}$ all negates. I'm here's savior.

Shattering shocks the is,   dares the dec,line of our race$_{\text{racy sex w/ siblings}}$ ·
At this stare Lolya's $_{\text{scandalized if eager}}$ eyes stare. But   Antigone recalls
Gilt glow-in-dark   stars,   eyes in   mouths. Georgi   myths.

Evening sinks. Enter Feodorus, pity, stranger, pity. Tones.
Enter Ferdin, plot, pitiless wall. Calls Antigone starved $_{\text{begged her}}$ de
    graded,
Calls for battle, dares threats. Bets on $_{\text{un}}$ gods.

A   blanching ·   mess,enge,r
Sees Grigori sees empty hubris of father, father-figure: t,win dearth.

His sister went with known cursed man $_{\text{I'm}}$ Georgi to distance,
now lets   she   Fer,din take her, $_{\text{sleeps,}}$ night   h,owls   flow,er
now t,urns back $_{\text{in}}$to   out,cast   by com$_{\text{e}}$passion. Cf. Feo,do$_{\text{lo}}$r,us.

This s,hit-matted hair, his/hers, fil,th and death w,or,ms.
Now he   Georgi   st,ands with sob,er feet, silver$_{\text{Jew?}}$ strained.
(The dead ones' $_{\text{step to death}}$ will seep to her from a cold bare room.)

Oh Father! Fired $_{\text{up, fiery,}}$ the mid,night way wrecks her, Georgi.
Disconnect   from$_{\text{with}}$ wrestle, siblings' slogans,   her shifting
    eyes despairing.
Our childish fear of death of fa$_{\text{r}}$ther$_{\text{undergod?}}$. Absent.
Sick, $_{\text{stunt}}$stunned, sh,all we negate   our   selves? H,is empty g,rave.

Leave this willing? But her yellow mood a child's mood? Ge,orgi's
   mouth.
Over   the f,ever   sheets of   young   angling: self-silence$_{violence}$?
Her grave not yet found. Her body, leitmotiv.

3 *Versus*

Grave   destiny th   inks ^Anti,gone: we went/go d own.
But   t,end, er ^Grigori, help me   bury Ge,orgi! Grigori:
Un   der blue   b,rows of ^our fath,er, ^his   fault,   we   can't!
Antigone: my   br,other   leads ^me, I   fol,low, honor him.   Leave me!
Antigone c,overs   naked Georgi. The dirt gets brushed off.   There are cries.
Man,kind   lines up   against the   b old   ^girl with her angel ^dust,
The   flesh of the   ^brother-saint   melts.

Meanwhile, Ferdin boasts royal purple: ^I am   the law, the overlord!
Two brot,hers' ends   sounding   my not-yel,lowed ^life-f,or,ce.
Flight ^to false war paths, humming of ^Georgi, Lyudovik.
But the resurrected ^don't meet on stone paths. Evening ^of such idols.

Antigone: Lepers, ^outcasts, mirror each other in   b,lack water.
^I o,pen ^my shit-flecked garment ^to him; I'm al,ready   dead.   You're not.
Grigori weeping ^as death's   stench wafts. Ferdin: *I'm the man, the over,man!*

Sl,end,er maid,ens g,rope, touch, key in th,rough nigh t's alleys,
trying to   find   no,bility. She's a heroine! Ob,serves loving ^Haamon.
You sound ^pussy-whipped, soft ^on h,er song, snarls Ferdin.

Let the ^we,dding song ^co,ver, re,member   , con,jure the boy, ^my be   loved,
My brother. His madness,   and   white brows and   his demise: ^Antigone.
The   ^wasted,   decayed   one w,ill bluely o,pen his eyes   ^to me.
Oh how sad, this seeing again. ^Our reunion.

The stages of   madness   in black   rooms.   ^Stage them.
Old shadows   un,der the open   do,or: ^Moira haunts and taunts Ferdin,
While the alien's soul watches itself in the ^gray mirror. ^You and your big ideas. *I'm the
   prophet.*

S,now and le,prosy   f,all   from   ^someone's   forehead.

157

The stars on the w,alls   have gone out,
And the   white figures   of night-light.   The shape of nothing   licks.

We lie   on the carpet, his boner rising   from some   g,raves. This is mine.
Silence.   Falling.   Ruined, addicted, declined, lapsed,
degenerated.
Victorino, Haamon, same-sad, find her.   Nightwind's sweetness. They don't cop,y;
          live.

You bro   ken eyes s,mashed in   b   lack mouths,
Wh,ere the   ungirl, grandchild in now gentle, soft   derangement
A,lone   swinging into darker end reflects on the toward/aftersense. She a   Nachlass.
Elsewhere, noncompos so-called Mother   lowers blue   lids. Necklace.

*

FROM HIS-TO-HER EARLY LOWER SEX-ON-GOSPEL POEM MEANING SAVIOR/
HELLION
Written in December 1912 and January 2012, it is Trakl's long-faced
poem. The dreariest and most earnest I have written, as she said
to Wladek. It, too, fails. Falls. Because she was in high-land—high
on the *Sinngott, Syntaxgott, Tongott.* It's claimed that Ryan Mariel
Rickie wrote to Lew Fletcher about the *inner intervals, pauses,* and
limits embracing, rubbing, kissing the *infinitely wordless.* Are my silent
spaces finite, worthless?

ANSWER KEY/LEGEND/HINTS (BECAUSE SHE'S EASY—I MEAN, I AM)
Moira = daughter of self-slain Lars, secret (tweener) mother of
Anton, also later of Georgi and Antigone, later of Haamon. Clearly
it's her tragedy, too. Anton's is denial. Trilogy's is Eros, Thanatos,
melancholia not mourning, Eternal Return of repressed. It's better,
more poignant, if you know the origins, sources.

I AM NOT A POET
I am not my brother. Instead do *Verwandlung der Pussy?* Or—?

*

VERWANDLUNG: GS PROSA/TRANSFORMATION: G'S PROSE
Winter: black shards. Am forest room. Stammer colder. Instant

destruction. The off flesh of an outcast is the sternum. Calling tree.
Long past amends. Stifles mussed minds. November's over. Now is
over. A clock loiters and the hurt fears a hairdo of black and written
perversions in permits. Under the hassle, God bush voids her green
yes-gear. Wild-out vs. white-out. His/her hands smell of smoking.
Veins bleed. And the shattered despair leaps over. Done eyes of the
Männchen/Mädchen/Mönchin: prone, silent. Dare woods. Crayons that
destroy themselves. Three: black, blue, yellow. Add white to get gray.
Her fuck equals a sonata. Fall verbs and bleached chords. Masculine
despair. Lies lost. Sick. One golden cloud auf'd. By the mewling, sin.
A girlboy struts. A fire. Johnny Strum-and-Stress. Johnny the Human
Torch. Flame is the palest brother laughing hisher grave into his
perpetrator hair. Odor is a door of murder: on the stoned way of the
past. The ball-bearings sinned and vanished. Longer hair dreamed in
belier's near air under the foreign forehead. Angst, green thoughts,
the gurgling of a drowning kid. Out of the starred vying unzips a
fissure, a gross black fault. Countenance of cruelty utters madness.
The voice of the reader. Hateful maiden in rucksack shocking the
one who is read, conned. Swollen, small. Over end of freedom, chest.
Wasted. Living in dunked sayings, hisher sex and the eyes stony
over nights and young girl's shirking. Task of done. Base evil. Metal.

What swings you to stand still on the vain fallen steps in the hours of
your father? Blackness fearing. What do you heap with sibling hand
on the blackness? And the lids sink like drinks from meaning. A
bare dirty mouth of stone. You see the starry sky in the milky street.
Saturnine rot. Razored mouth. Undone from stone. Clapped the cold
branch. You on the fallen stage: bro, sis , stone. Mark of exclamations.
You, a blue deer that cites lies, trembles. You, the bleak presto that
slaughters its hints on the black alter-ego. You're licking the dark,
sad and evil prose, a kid blanches in sleep. A red flame sprang
from your handwriting and a faltering night burned her daring. O
faltering lights, the flattering dead. What swings you still to stand
on the fallen steps in the hows of your father? Downstairs, from the
tower door, an angle. Christ names your doubtful finger.

O the hell of sleep; dark guest, burned Gretchen. A dead feminine
shape loiters lightly to blur evening. Small green flowers, gawking.
And her face has left her. Or it naysays, pale over the cold brow

of the murderer in the darkness of hothouse flowers. Adoring
unbuttoning purple time of lust. His sister, bent, stumbles down the
black steps of the proof into darkness.

That man left you at the crossroads, and for a long time you look
back. Siblings' steps in shades of crumpled apple. Poem, keychain.
Perpetual light from black guest, feared and in grass, insane Swiss/
sweat. Treads on the icy forehead and the sad dreams in cries, in the
door, shrinking. Under black despising, Greta balks. You, still wild,
the red island, music from brow cigarette-smoke-clouded, and from
the inner, the wild shame of Gretchen. Lift notes into the sea, storm,
stress, ice. You, a groaning metal and inside, a fiery visage that
wants to go and ink from hooked legs, dark signs, and the flaming
stuttershirt of narrowness. O! despair, that with a stammered shout
breaks its knees.

A dead man visits you. From his chest suicidal blood runs and an
unspeakable moment nicks his black brow. Dark encounter. You—a
purple mouth, as he appears green in shadow of fig tree. From which
follows a never-past night.

Method Not-Acting
Consult the list of supererogatory duties such as Nietzsche vs.
Trakl, Grete's full bio, Franz, Liz Taylor and Monty Clift, Gregoire
or Gregor, fairy tales, the picture theory of propositions/poems, the
correspondence theory of truth, bilingualism.
Insult the duty of supererotic listing: incest semantics, expression in
art, feeling metaphysics, labyrinthine wandering. I cannot see what I
am doing.
Voice of his now a constant, black noise. If this could make it white
noise? Or white it out? But no innocence.
Greta's contribution in a secret composition book—a transnotebook
that wore a gray cover. Question of poetical/sexual identity not
solved by a flowery tie. Is paisley flowery? If it's on your face, it
is leprosy. Thus hide at home, do not go to the reading or bank to
display your voice or deposit or withdraw money so you can eat and
keep living. The right place would be a high floor or that school/
university building. But now it's the Geneva mental hospital. The
Swiss Institute offered an unrelated victor too far away. Erector set.

Vector. Language sidles off if you aren't true to it. The language says, start a new paragraph, maybe I will return to you and love you. Or a girl does.

Dirt under the fingernails does not entail manual typewriter labor. It could signify a death wish. Hamlet or Antigone redux.

Obsession with the suicide pact idea as a word problem involving time, distance, acceleration.

First a cripple with legs that curled and looked metallic like a saw, then a cripple with legs that jutted and seemed wooden like a plank: both used canes. The sky with clouds and golden light you can love but not show your face to. So she folded it up, thrust into the pocket of her tight jeans and continued on, a puncture wound in space-time.

Nietzsche vs. Schopenhauer.

Greta's marriage to Ferdek; the details.

Trauma, derangement; *Family Affair* with Byron Keith.

Haakon, her younger brother, did mechanical procedures involving chance and chains of mistranslations. His technical/aleatoric vs. her existential/narcissitic poetics. So Greta didn't have sex with him like with Georg, nor with him and Georg at the same time.

I am not sure what should happen now.

Wounds of the ideas are unstaunchable instantiations. Ideation. Unshaved armpits. Expressionist first personal hygiene like an Austrian *Mädchen* in 1914?

Can I Be Excused? May I Please Be Excused Now? Title of never-to-be-written novel!

How hard is it to put that thing in your mouth, curl your finger? Become the OverGreta? The It'sAllOverGreta? *Die Verwandelte.*

WITH FERDL, I SAY: DON'T FEEL SORRY FOR ME!

My brother and my sister-in-law are now reading me with pity and perhaps scorn.

*

PALE GRAY UNCOMPOSED NOTEBOOK / ALSO SCORED GRETA THURSTAN
As Georg also Greta

as Greta same-said awakened

Ill as when as whereas Georg

feels a weird pressure

                                     word pressure

Never faced this corner before

My metallic body pale green like the death of underpainting

                             leprous corrosion of rosy skin

Or silver-white metallic

Liquid is

                metaphysical liquids

                   How morphine into

                            fluid or flow

Although he did crystal method

                     over does the brother

                        douse or dose

Sister sounded liquid

            changing easily yet metallic

Ergo Mercury aka Hermes then w/ the love also, aphrodisiac

                     metaphysics

       Was Grete a hermaphrodite?

                   Her mental dick

               My metal lick

This phallic metallic

    or tastes blood the same blood her/my husband's idea

St. Januarius was before he met Lou, who destroyed him, he

                      resurrected himself

But spurn his pathos

          accident comedy vs. substance comedy

          substance monism

          illegal substance monism

As when awoke from restless troubled uneasy worried

figment

noisy dreams   *sans* fig leaf or daydreams was she sleeping
during the day

again intoxicated, high

intoxicant idealism, addictive idealism, chemical idealism

It is all so chemical or like the chemistry we shared myself and my
brothers myself and my sister-in-law myself and my father

Once your breast is broken
unchaste chest organ

Also broke Greta Thurstan

I never did this before   like this

unknowing

the white disc of the table almost too small for the metallic
meanings

Morose morph morpheme morphia morphine morphology

How the word *is* the body, their illogic

my beautiful brother Georg his logos
Georg meaning farmer as in husbandry
therefore Ferdl as Grete's *husband* a fraud

Then mercury stayed fluid in the room
at room temperament

Have they locked me in a detox? This asylum

As Greta Thurstan awoke one twilight from uneasy
                              when they say that she was easy
               numbing vs. goading

         the sweet brother/pond whispered narcotic idealism
         the sharp sister/whirlpool retorted stimulant idealism!

weren't identical twins
weren't fraternal twins

                         is the type of woman who gives women a bad
Like vampire!

Awoke as Georg

                              while Greta is the vampire
                              or Lulu

So tired of being alone, without him
                              do you understand?
                              oh brother and sister

                    substance abuse dualism
                    I his narcotic, he my stimulant
                    he my tic, I his *Antlitz*

Grete and Georg's overlap

          in her lap he put his face trip or tripping

          meanwhile Friedrich Ferdl Ferdek Ferdinand

Syphilitic and megalomaniacal vs. leprous

                    mercury used for skin infections
                    the skin a love organ
                    I play, also the piano and
                    this other keyboard

Ferdek would improvise for hours, put himself into a trance or intoxicated state

                    inebriation idealism

At some point, you leave the notes beyond, no, behind, quit scoring,
play new notes impulsive

          Fetzen means rag, scrap, shred, fragment, bit, snatch,
          Fetzig means wild like Greta/Grete not like e.g. Lola/Lolya

                    fawn fox raven   from the brothers' fairy tales
                                                      or poems, stories

                    replaces Fritz's *Kamel* or the sleazy camel cigarettes
                    but leopard would be closer to *Löwe*. And to leper!
                    And *Kind* = kid

                              I hope this doesn't destroy me, everything
                              I destroy like Grete with my character's
                              boner handwriting with the sharp *Spitzen*
                              nails

          didn't want to be numb
                                        then something

What am I doing in this room?
They are all outside of it.

As my words taste blood like the test of the door, its key, I can't get
the mixed typing writing prose poetry ergo in labyrinth

                    not quite ready to stop but have to stop
                              do I still have an hour?

          can't get my head out of this bed, my bed out of this head

                    Can only think of sex around me: hypocrite, tease!
                    Or as if all girls do is give each other head! Please!
                    Shall I demo how we'd fuck?

Cf. Georg's hostile Grete unnerved
by his poet friend, mannish Jewish
Else Masker-Schwuler!

Skin not always a disease

can cause unease uneasy daydreams dream days
vainglorious

Snatches

from the clutches of clichés are deaths.

*

It was how the sound builds slowly. And after so much quiet, sounds
impossibly loud.

A sound has volume only in the context of a sequence

but the stillness
not like death, deathly
shit caked in the sisters' hair?

He says they go off to the old men

bare, leafless rooms

As Greta Thurstan awoke one dusk from

grown too hard my armor
Tired of this room

then Greta Thurstan wanted to go out
but she couldn't stand up, even sit, it
gave her vertigo, entailed edge of
mountain, cliff, abyss, strophe

the high-pitched tone under the deep voice

I am a boy, my voice is changing!
They said, I like your high, girlish voice,
But they lied.

The unruly dream, to think you could avoid turning into your
brother

      he was with golden sores glowing on his pale skin
        his madness sat on his white chest
         his back when he departed
          the sister lies in the empty room of her brother

I have to get up, thinks Greta; I have to get out of here

        Scored for piano, dark flute, vibraphone, chimes
        Moves slowly, lacking tension

    The collection of notebooks spread out
    Or mean it was all the same notebook, referent, but w/
    different senses
    or w/ synonyms
    Or partial synonyms as the senses interpenetrate in idiolects
    bounded yet open like worlds inside you except

      Our inside-out skin our infectious influx in fucks

They said counterfactual
               subjunctive as if Georg hadn't

I don't know how to
do this I don't know how to
any more I
don't
know more
I

It was a traveler, wanderer, *Wanderleben*

             The picture a photo from
             their wedding or an author
             photo I mean translator I
             mean they will move my
             body when it is a corpse,

won't you, dear brother and
sister?
The street like sandpaper to rub you raw
I would like to rub
you raw your awe
our war or *war*

I would like to rub
out do erasure

use a rubber not get
pregnant

The young woman with my brother draped all over her
unless the inverse
pet a pelt
My brother Gregor hirsute
or a snake

she is disappearing into the beast animalistic
all over me like a dead thing skin

my writing desk is too small and white my

chest my body
my weak chest which as always

Now w/ teen acne
I am turning into a boy!
Turning into a vampire!
Into a knight in shadow armor
Into a leper
Into a phrase that sounds rushed, forced, unclean

my feelings
their words
their syntax

I do not want my feelings.

I want a system to avoid, spurn my

feelings
Ferdinand?

She ran away from him.
Tonight a literary party
It said their storm
came down from a high to find herself lying
I can hear, but I hear only ringing. In my ears, not outside them.

Supposed to be a dream. Now a rant.

my italic hair

I could not keep everything, the world, in my mind
so parts of the world went quiet, withered, died

spaced-out idealism

Does the world die in the pauses?

Versus how six made their way in the world. Greta and her five
beloved brothers.

Why is that here?

And the sister-in-law should not be here.
Is she the father or the sister figure of my brother Gregor's novella?
As Greta Thurstan awoke one evening, she found herself turned into
her brother's novella.
It was thin, rusty-yellowish, lay on its back.
Nobody wanted to touch it, read it. Still wet. Her ink would stain
them.
I promised, I will avoid the pathos! But I lied.

*

Will to remake
Eternal reverse
Übermädchen

Will to make out?

and first personalism, to replace Ferdinand's perspectivism
oh, I have ideas!

Eternal reverse is oscillation. Our metaphysical essence.

Sempiternal would only be temporal. But the oscillation

> beyond time, but in time.
> eternal and temporal: the incarnation.
> but not what happens after you die
> but don't you return?

> Fraternal return

>> I saw my
>> haunted brother
>> ghostly brother

>> the bell rang
>> it went off in her head
>> she went off her head or in it

too many uppers/downers
it was the head brother
the principal or most valuable brother

> the authorized representative brother
> the procurer
> the representational author brother
> the lead brother, or the leaden one

>> to get possession of, obtain
>> to make women available for promiscuous
>>> sexual intercourse
>> to achieve

procure prod prodigy prodigal

god
a god
goad
the good

suddenly disappeared into a room and

shoots herself full of lead

Now the leading role or plays the lead or *das Lied*

knowing good in evil

too much stimulant!

serpent

their father's prick   or was it the brother's?

The same brother? Or an older brother?
Such as Gregor? He liked to watch this.

But the fall is philosophical. Compose it.

Übermädchen. Übermaß. Don't be such a sissy!

sssssssssssssssssssssshhhhhhhhhhhhhhhhhhsssss

mmmmmm

tatatata   ta   ta

                        fhh   fhh

                   errrrrrrrrrrrrrrrrrrrr ch

         hhhmmmmmmmmmmmmmmmmm

                         eeeeeeeeeeeeeeeeee
eeeeeeeeeeeeeeeeeeeeeeeeeeeee

fhuuh   fhuuh

                            sssssshhhhh

wait

My dream his derangement his dream my derangement my and his
pt. 2 of his poem pt. *n* of my notebook is our *and* and our private
privat und unsere und:

       liebte
If meaning and truth   not the same, but love   can't live w/o each
   verbrannte   *Unzucht*   *dammernden Zimmern*
other. Incest semantics!   Also sentence and world. Girl expression,
   blaue   *erstarren Tür*   *die nächtige Gestalt*
brother world. Then girl world, brother expression. Both as truth. Its
  Zu   *Schatten des Bösen.*
trinity: reality, veracity, fidelity. A sibling or the papa. Paper! Rib
    ihr Nächte und Sterne.
uluation unguent instrumental   lubricates thinking. They say not
  Am Abend   *Krüppel Berge*   *eisigem Gipfel*   *Glanz der Abendröte*
ontological, neither true nor false, but that's wrong. My tool is real!
  Schwer schwanken die stürmischen   *und der rote*   *trat aus dem Wald.*
To produce new predications, predilections, techniques is to make a
    Nacht   *zerbrach kristallen*   *die Finsternis schlug deine Stirne.*
poem. W/ sets and possible worlds. But not because useful or avoids
    kahlen   *erwürgte*   *eisigen Händen*   *eine wilde*
contradictions like   sound wave vs. white powder. Rather because
 Klagend weisse Gestalt eines Engels,   *wuchs im Dunkel der Schatten*
significant. Hurts, doesn't help you live, have   control, but it is
 Stein *warf ihn er heuland floh* *seufzend*   *Baums*   *sanfte Antlitz*
true. Then incest metaphysics of I and world. Each I its world   but
   Lange lag er   *und sah staunend das goldene Zelt der Sterne.*
also faces it. Rubs it. Twins. The velcrocosm! And to love the world
   Chased by bats, *stürzte*   *fort ins Dunkel.*
of your brother, the brother-world, too! So it becomes yours. Then
     Atemlos stepped *er ins verfallene haus.*
moments when you and the world fuse, become one, as in true sex.
    trank er, ein wildes Tier   *blauen*   until
Sister and brother one being.   The many brothers; you should love
 Fierbend eisige Stiege, ranting   God   he would die.
all of them. But you love one more.   Incest poetics: to touch, love the
   das graue Antlitz des Schreckens,   *Augen*   *zerschnittener* throat
brother's words.   Georg sounds like the other Georg when he was

Rushing *fremde*   *Judenmädchen griff her* black *Haar*   took her mouth.
grasping the hell of the other, as his ersatz.   Lends parataxis.   Now
  Enemies *folgte ihm*   dark alleys   iron clattering.
Trakl down affect! Instrument for achieving affect. Musical measures
       herbstlichen   *schweigenden   verdorrten*   trees drunk
to display de- and vice. Instrumentation equals orchestration.   Or
                    die verfallene disc *der*
castration. Frustration. Gustation. Instrumental solipsism: the world
            Süße torments *verzehrten* his flesh.
is my performance!   But trans and incest?   Translit metaphysics?
   In   halfway house *erschien* to him *starrend*   filth his bleeding figure.
No time for that. Ellipsis vs. solipsist. A lipped sis.   Worlds rub in
 liebte tower *höllischen* nightly *blauen Sternenhimmel* cool   fiery   kept
sexed intersection. To be in his/your   set w/ shared   members.
      Weh, der unspeakable *Schuld,*   manifests.
When worlds collide. Co-lewd, glide   off. In risqué contact of close,
 glowing fall   walked *unter*   in cloak of her hair *flammender* demon sister
connected. Our sibling art   is the expression   of reality   as fled.
       Upon waking, went out   *ihren* heads.

                              *

        through the window a   mental hospital
                                                military hospital

            reverberation of destroyed sense

                              destructive
                              dented chest sonata

our voice
             my brother's voice possessed meds
I hear the cure   in the fuck shirt

              superderogatory   the morning fog
                                        the mourning fuck

                                           ash, ashen

Greta, the procurer is here   I know muttered to itself what is knowing?

the mental hospital is not
hospital green like my piano
that would be clichéd
the mental hospital is violet
the military hospital is purple

brother's blood translated into crimson
brilliant would be mocked locution

this is I am not going anywhere, still merely lying down

too low to fellatio

fellate   late   bro

waiting for him to come to me, weigh me down, come on me, but
now he is weightless

wait, again
feel@brother

*

It missed Thor's day because paralysis   sis too exhausted to leave
the bed

is this freedom?

Bare your head, its thorny hair,
black and gray upper parts, rusty-yellow feet.
Legs, hands, arms, ears.

her corroded sonic intervals

now a systematic:

Gregor Samsa = Greta

Grete Samsa = sister-in-law Lola
father = friend Wladek
mother = brother Haakon
serving girl = brother Gregor
chief clerk = brother Georg
cook = brother Ludvik
cleaner = brother Victor
three lodgers = three alpha male poets
(conceptualist, pop cultist, performance artiste)

use the story to run away from the window, the window
from the story?

Ludvik, you were supposed to take me with you!
You fed me, made me tomato sandwiches, the same every day.
Tormented me when I was in school.
I was natural and spontaneous, did not get bogged down in
philosophy.
Then one day I awoke transposed into a passive troubled boy.
But you like boys! Well, only some boys. The strong carefree healthy
ones.
Please leave, I do not want your philosophy anymore anyway.

> hysterical symptoms are made up, invented
> hysterics are creative!

> even though *invented* means found

I can't sit up, can't stand, walk, dance. I cannot eat. They think I am
repulsively thin.

The theory of language is also a metaphysics. Morphology as
ontology. The idea of morphing. Transmutations.

> mutate vs. mute

This was supposed to be philosophy. Then it got aggressive.

I am not my saintly poetic genius brother Georg!

So when I awoke to find myself turning into him, I was a horror.

Rant here—about what?
                                             but I am too flat and tired

                    Please, Greta! Please complete something.

                    Please explain your philosophy
                    finally, once and for all!

I can't explain nor yet describe it, but I can exclaim it and do it—w/ free love.

        is that slut metaphysics? easy lay logics

                    Eternal reverse is God the father.
                    Will to remake is God the son.
                    Übermädchen is God the holy spirit/ghost/sister.

                    But the fall? Oh yes, explain the fall.

                    The fall as escape from the room. Once upon a time,
                    we were velvet ones. Then something   intervened.

                                    *

Here is how the fall works: No! Instead do a fairy tale.

How Six Remade the World in Their Way
Once upon a time there was a girl named Greta who had only one skill—she could run fast. With her leg of argument unglued so she wouldn't run too fast. Faster than the speed of speed or coke. Had fought in a private argument with correction fluid and courage but the war was over, she was discharged like a premise, provisional assumption, and received only three propositions for her travails. Just wait, she said. I will inhabit the kingdom! Treasure is the revaluation. Trading for the one pearl of great posse. Pussy! Pries loose. Passes apace.

Full of rage, she turned into a forest and there saw a hunky leafy-haired man tearing up as he tore out six trees like sheets of paper. The world is my door/notebook. Will you serve as my brother Haakon and travel with me? Yes said the young man, but first I want to bring the trees to my mama. Because he was a gentle man, a caring son. We two shall certainly remake the world in our way.

Next a hunter was kneeling because modest, taking aim at something. The fly in the fly bottle. On the tree of form of life's branch. Look carefully. Come with me, if we three are brothers, said Greta, we'll certainly remake the world in our way.

The hunter, Ludvik, had a will that was the world's, so he went with. Seven windmills spinning. Then a lanky man perched like a jackdaw on a tree. He, Gregor, was breathing with difficulty. What are you up to? I'm breathing out so the windmill blades turn. Oh come be my brother! If we four stick together, we'll certainly remake the world in our way.

So the blower came down and they went along. Then a young man, Victor, was standing on two legs. He had mastered many skills (like Novalis) and conducted himself correctly. Oh become with me my brother. If we five adhere to the story, we shall certainly remake the world our way. So he went with them, and then another man came with a felt army cap cocked on his head. Where are your manners, you should remove your cap! I can't, if I do, a tremendous frost comes and freezes all the birds or girls. Oh come with me as my brother Georg. If we six etc., then etc. the world.

Now the city. The king Sigismund. His daughter Lili. Whoever wins the race can be her Georg. No, her mate. But whoever loses will lose his head. The fast girl sent the young man who'd mastered many skills to say he wished to race by proxy, through a servant. The king: So both your lives may be forfeited. Ok. Then the masterful young man buckled Greta's missing limb onto her and said, Now show us how fast you are, and help us all win!

The running girl and the king's daughter were given fly bottles and started running together. Yet within moments, the runner was gone, for she blew away like the wind. Soon hit the river, filled the bottle (putting the fly out of its misery), and spun around. But halfway back, she was overcome by fatigue or just distraction, lay down and daydreamed. For her pillow she took a thick metaphysical book that had grown in the forest, so she wouldn't become too comfortable in a deep sleep. Meanwhile the king's daughter, who was also unusually fast, comes rushing back with her water. When she sees the other girl lying down, she empties that one's bottle and resumes running. All would have been lost, except that the hunter/remarksman had been standing on top of a ladder outside the castle and saw everything that was the case with his sharp eyes. I will make sure that female does not defeat us. And he loaded his weapon and fired at the fat speculative book so it shot away. The girl Greta awoke and saw the other girl was ahead and had undone her, emptied her out. But she did not lose courage, ran back to fill her bottle again, then raced forward and managed to beat the girl with two pages to spare. You see, she said, it was about time I saw how fast I could really go. It shouldn't exactly be called running what I did before. Well what determines that? It doesn't matter. Call it whatever you like, said Ludvik the marksman, as long as you know what's at stake. But the king was perturbed, and his daughter more so, that a girl, a 98-lb weakling instead of a Polish nobleman or superman, had won the race. So they shut the five brothers and the one sister in a room of iron with delicious food as bait. Then they made the cook Wladimir start a fire under the room to heat them. But the young man Georg with the military cap said, Oh, I shall let a frost come and end all the heat. So he removed his cap, and from his bared head the whole area grew not freezing but cool. Thus the six survived in the room until the king went to let them out. He was aggravated. So he offered all the gold one could lift in the place of his too-beloved daughter Lili to the young master of many skills, who agreed. Two weeks of packing later, the strong man, the one built like a tree with legs like trees, could still carry the sack, no worries. And more and more treasures and gold went into the sack, but he, Haakon, could handle it all, it did not weigh him down or paralyze him. Finally there was nothing left out but still room in the sack when he said, Let's get going.

When the king's daughter saw how fine and strong Haakon was, she secretly jumped into the sack so he would carry her with him.

And no one knew, and the six plus one headed off. But once the king realized his Lili had deceived him, he sent an army of supermen after the six plus one to get her back. Let go of the princess, or you'll be cut to pieces! What, whispered the blower Gregor, we are your prisoners? Before that happens, you'll all be flopping like book leaves in the air. With that, he took a deep breath and exhaled toward the soldiers. It made a musical piping noise. And scattered them every which way, while one young soldier begged for mercy. Since he was brave and wounded and did not deserve to be humiliated (his name was Samson), the breather spared him. He said, Now go to the king and tell him if he sends any more of a regimen I will blow it up. When the king received the message, he said, Let the six ones go with my girl. There's something superexceptional about them. So the six brought their wealth of world back and divided it amongst themselves. And the brother Haakon and the princess Lili lived happily until and even after her, Greta's, death. While she went faster to her private finish line.

The world is made of air, said Gregor.
The world is made of ice, said Georg.
The world is made of trees, said Haakon.
The world is made of magic, said Victor (who renamed himself Vincenzius).
The world is made of gamesmanship, said Ludvik.
The world is made of movements, said Greta.

*

Then she wrote,   *I am wholly and utterly broken and hunted*
                     like an animal

                     I am utterly and completely smashed and
                     hounded, as a beast

                     shaken, not stirred anymore, ever.

                     It was on the tongue, groove

                     How the emo versus the classical

Mad look in sister's eyes: *zerüttet*
Long hippie hair, she could be the 1970s and drugs

Georg did them to flee,
did she do them to expand her consciousness?
Greta and Georg did it to flee,
did they do it to expel their consciousness?

I'm getting a cigarette from my room
It was her new unhome in the storm

But the marks on the photo: blood, splatter
pattern, decay or corrosion, my silver-plated
fleshed-out face, flushed from fucking fate's
punctuation

Greta caught leprosy from Grete,
prosody from Georg,
then the picture constellation
has no shirt on

Sister and brother saw each other in the garden

Her right eye broken, left eye hunted
Right eye resentful, left eye sad
Right manic, left depressed
Right coked up, left doped up

Some sort of *bild* in
the background, not
a theory

Out of focus landscape or outer world?

Grete or Greta not subtle

She *ein sterbender Jüngling* says Georg, or Jeanne Dark not d'Arc,
not in their war. Little girl playing the piano *as if possessed*, Grete's
middle name Jeanne

Hearing notes not voices. Or *his* voice?

If you grow up speaking your brother's
language, his tongue in your mouth

It's the mouth and nose that are angry,
rapacious

He wrote wolf in his poem, I wrote fox

In the picture, the young lady's wearing a fox stole, fox hat, fox
muffler; which girl is Grete Trakl, which is Greta? Or it's Georg?

In the Prater, Ludvik picked up young men, rough trade,
brutish, but Georg and Greta picked up shadows. Had their
twinning silhouettes done. Put the dark pictures here, face to
face? That's uncountenanced.

Grew up kissing French. But Catholic guilt and the saint idea.

I think I will become a translator, vowed Grete /
Greta

please amuse my mouth
in the park, in the garden

I think I will become a well-known translator for a
frank publishing house after my last battle

I mean an unknown translated

It's cheerful and relaxing when you finally make a decision

The fall is the fall. Likeness leaves? Leaf, through.

An opisthograph is a manuscript or book having
writing on both sides of the leaves.
The leave has two sides, where Georg and Grete are
written.

Opisthograph   opium   opiumism

Where did she get the equipment? I am sure she got it from her dead brother. His weapon, pistol. How it shoots. Then she was packing.

The heat wasted on Georg, he was cold. But her?

Wasting away. Also like Gregor. Though here, he is the manservant. Oh, is it time for that story? I thought it was still time for a theory of the fall.

It's the fall. I am cold now. There isn't much time left.

Monk-girl, un-Saint Jeanne, Grete
light and dark. I can't help it if the
same references recur. They are
addictive.

You can tell she wants to eat you.

That's what they say about Greta.
Am I a brute? Am I brute?

One dusk, Greta Samson awoke to
find herself turned into a brutality

my beloved little demon
is that he or I?

I need more drugs
I am running out of drugs

What does *Salettl* mean?
Little room, so little,
salacious, slut all,
slit ill, islet,
the let all,
saw lit hell,
sell it all

for one taste
die taste / *die Taste*
judgment of sublime
or of beauty
critique
her critical nostrils
large and flared like his
they shared one appetite
lupine but cervine

First he's the fawn, she's the wolf, then the inverse.
But he never became the fox.
I think she is little and a vixen—
aggressive woman, foxy girl or vexing sister—

Greta as ill-tempered clavier

You literary demon!
With flaming hair.
It was red when Greta was a girl. Then it turned darker.

Futile to try to flee the curse. This

should stay it.

will to unmake, eternal reverb, *Untermädchen*

my useless effort to find my husband attractive

now I could shoot myself at the sex party titled Submit

but I won't do that
I will / want to be original

Pearl gray faintly bluish dildo

feral, dusky?

There were two leaves, and their
names were written on them

No
There was one leaf, and their
groins were pushing on it,
its two opposite sides
So the leaf was held between them, but
they had to stay pressed together,
crotch to crotch. If they drew apart,
the two-sided leaf would fall and they
would see everything, the nothing
But it's hard to hold it in place if
she grows wet and slippery, and he gets
hard, erect, or she gets hard, erect,
he grows wet and slippery—

The fall

*

2ND VERSION: *AUS DER FASSUNG, SICH ZU FASSEN* / UNNERVED, TO COMPOSE
ONESELF
Psalm: the sound made by striking, touching, plucking, rubbing,
twanging, or vibrating, perhaps with the hands or fingers, mostly of
musical strings

Psalm/Lapse

1 Now it is the creeping of my
brother Gregor. Sometimes
subtly creepy. It is his question
to the girl, Did Father say not
to read each tree? A garden that
means enclosure, garden. Their
little house next door, barbaric
with ink black milk. It is there is.
Ist, isst. Georg stammers in the
child-sized house, eat-in Eden.
Eden means delight. *Paradise*
means park, pleasure-grounds.
Dark *Licht* in the enclosure.
2 Greta said, We may eat of the
fruit of the trees of the garden as
a room of white milk, burning,
3 but of the black *Loch* which is
the middle, God said, Do not
eat or touch it, or you'll die. The
mad ones will die.
4 Gregor said, You won't die.
5 He is not God: our Father.
When you eat, your eyes shall
be opened, and you will be like
Dad, knowing good and evil.
God and nausea. Goth and bad.
Please do not undo my belt. *Bad*
means hermaphrodite in the

originality. Is cut short. Each the twin of the other. Or they could fuse into one. Georg and Grete: sons of God ready to receive. Fangs. The tree of knowledge a hermaphrodite of good and evil in the garden. Why in the garden? To test the boy and girl? Like with a blue octavo notebook for the in-class text I will write, says Gregor. The tree of life and the tree of knowledge were in the garden but not *of* it. Like you: in, not of your body, whispers Gregor. Although pleasant to the sight and good for food. For thought, as of the father who roamed there. While his wife / their mother stays sad inside, polishes her objects. The tree had apples such as the story of Gregorius by Hermann von Eye, which Gregor transmuted into his novella *Die Verwandlung*. How that apple is thrown at you by the father, sticks in you and hurts you, how repellent, creeping you are. You, the first born, made in his image—so he hates you. In the garden, the younger brother and sister, Georg and Greta, were free. Harmonized in music. They perform *Tänze* Gregor doesn't understand. But they share his G. Ogling their own genitals with glee, he alone with guilt. Girl called Ishmael, boy called *ich*. Oh, is that bad,

hermaphrodite language? Or they reversed it, transposed poses, unafraid. Performed, swung hips. Delicate, passive, brutish, aggressive. Violent! Refined. *O unser velorenes Paradies*.
6 Then Greta saw that the tree looked good for food, was alluring, and desirable to make her wise, she stole its fruit because she is proud but gave a bite to her spacy brother Georg because she is generous. Then their eyes were made watchful like Gregor's, and they received the concept of naked; and they sewed leaves into loincloth books to hold over their crotches. The nymphos have left the golden woods. Where the stranger, the father, was buried. *Loin* means far or faraway in French, as Mademoiselle had taught them when they were Gothic as Frenching, age 12-16, pointed nipples arched back rib vaulting fine woodworking stonehard working, progressive dematerializing or 13-15. Or music played 12-14 years old. In lit, Goth is the gloomy setting, grotesque, mysterious or violent events, atmosphere of degeneration, decay. *Verfall*. Georg's atmospherics. His vapor. Her vapors? Ingenuous heroine, except always already she knew things. But not

how it was bad, depraved, degenerate. She was a small girl in the garden, wearing dresses of shocking skimpiness, often taking them off. Gregor watched her. Saw rooms feeling chords and sonatas, shadows embracing before a blind mirror. He a star and forehead, *Stern*, austere, mysterious but attractive, melancholic, oldest big brother. Like the father! Patient warming himself by sanatorium window. A damp pallor. Bloody cough. Goth like my city of the comic books my brother Victor showed me. Batman afraid of everything, but Robin, his little sister, isn't! Yes, she is. But that comes after. Which brother should you fear, which can you trust? What if you love all of them? A son of pain appears shaped as a bitter word. A strange sister appears in the young man's bad dreams. Resting there with her hazel brown bush, she plays with herself. With his star. The student, perhaps a double, watches her from his window. In front of him stands his soon-dead brother; he will descend. 7 *Es ist ein Fall* into the *Konzept* of naked, which is a judgment. Its form deformity: knowing, not feeling—of being w/o clothing on genitals or female nipples, blunt like the frank truth or bare fucked, unprotected (e.g. w/o a condom), uncomfortable as if suddenly missing something like the bro, other, brother. So a fall into separation from union. But what if the sister/rib sometimes *wanted* to get away from the brother, escape his enclosure, instead sleep on glowing asphalt, so she bit Gregor's book? But not out of shame, for the fall is *into* shame, the first shame, over your body and sexuality, and fear of being exposed as disgusting. Like Gregor, masturbating in the garden. Brown, not pale. Not a novice. The garden is night. The two children quit playing around, look for the sky's gold: Paradise. The father wished them to be free of guilt. But the girl did not want to be free of it out of naivete, or in a fantasy. Because she already knew things, was innocent yet experienced, and fairy tales, if they're any good, are also bad, two-toned, hermaphroditic. So she rebelled. But Georg felt shame and made her wear cacao and poppies and poppers on her pussy. Because he wished them to be naive children again. And now he fucked her differently. They had two languages, poetry and music, like the sibling creation myths, but after the fall were *I sh* (Hebrew man) and *I sh sh ah* (Hebrew young woman) because of the need for secrecy. So their knowing was a fallen feeling, their self-consciousness a curse. Recursive from the father, oldest brother. So now what? Chord of quartet. The small not-blind girl runs trembling through the All, the avenue, the lay, but that's later. When her cold shadow will rub the wall, she'll project their *Märchen* and holy gender-legends onto it.

8 So they heard their father's voice walking in the black garden at twilight, it was cold, they hid from his bleakness in the trees of the garden. He was dead. They, orphans.

9 And Dad called out, Where are you?

10 And Georg blurted, I heard your hollow voice in the enclosure and I was afraid, also because I was naked, so I hid myself.

11 And he said, Who told you to be afraid? Who uttered naked? Did you eat of the forbidden fruit?

12 And the brother said, It was my sister! She tempted me, and I ate.

13 And the father said, Greta, what did you do? And the girl said, My creepy other brother beguiled me, and I ate.

14 And the father said, Gregor, because you did this, you are cursed to crawl on your belly and choke on vapor daily.

15 And your sister won't love you anymore, your sayings won't be her sayings, she'll strikethrough your head, but you will remain her Achilles' heel.

16 To the girl he said, You will be Greta full of sorrow and painful conceptions, you'll desire your Georg and be ruled by him. His angelic dirt-flecked flicker will splatter your gray room.

17 And to Georg he said, Because you fell in love with the voice of your sister, and ate from Gregor's novella's truth tree when I commanded you not to, cursed is the ground of your subjectivity. In sorrow you'll eat of this ground your whole brief life.

18 Thorns and sister's thicket it will bring forth from you. And the snakelike brother with yellow lids will recur.

19 In this fear-sweat you'll crave a sisterbrother and return to powder. For out of dust you were made up, and to dust you'll return.

20 Georg called his sister evening, twilight. But she had already called herself Greta, because she had traded them all

for her self, it was pale gray.
21 Then the father threw his deathly cloak over them like a magician, and it became their second nature or skin and covered them. So they had his fashion, were modeled after him. Or like models in Bresson's films, how he would film Georg, Greta, Gregor and the father in the expulsion—with minimalism, restraint, vs. this childish heightening. And with a quartet, and silver shots of feet. But Greta, don't be self-conscious!
22 And the shadow of the father said to the shadow of his sister, They became one with us, distinguishing good from evil, and feeling shame. And they knew change and loss. Now they might keep rubbing together forever, just to live in the moment, not think about it. We should stop them. In truth, he couldn't bear to see them, now that they mirrored him.
23 So he drove the man out from the garden and *Salettl* to be Georg.
24 Expelled him to the past, where Mademoiselle aka the father's undead sister would flash her doctrine which blocked the way to the tree of life.
25 And now this exceeds the model, number, because it's a notation. Note how only the young man is become like them and cast out. The girl isn't mentioned. Maybe she is still in paradise or could be. Except that she wants to go back with her brother. Dive into his sighs. So she leaves Eden, too. Not banished: a runaway. Making his fate her character. Like when she played Ishmael, who, exiled, became a joyous wanderer, hisher arrow pointing everywhere.
26 What is the fall? It depends on its source. Gregor's fall came out of envy, Greta's out of pride, Georg's out of gluttony. So each fall was distinct. But linked by fantastic lust: *eine weisse Magd spielt mit Schlangen.* Near the man's/father's grave. But now, could Gregoire's I be God's eye and open itself, look elsewhere to an *Überschädelstätte*, transGolgotha?

*

MIDRUSH ON PSALM
It could be read differently! If the fall were good, like scales falling from eyes as for the gnostics via gnosis/know-sis, if Gregoire were the snake, and rebellion and knowledge led to a higher

truth, condition, of musical scales with twelve semigod tones
Greta qua Gregoire scrawled in the blue octave notebook, the fall
from immediacy into necessary rupture, but then to a superunion,
experienced but innocent, cf. the German Romantics, for in the
beginning sister and brother thought they were one and simple,
but they were different and complicated, then they ate Gregor's
cautionary story about the one who's utterly alienated from
his body, cannot express himself in it, because the others find it
disgusting, because it/he has fantasies of fusion of animal with
girl, because he loves his musical sister Grete, although he doesn't
understand her language, if you look at the body from outside, it
is only an object among objects, albeit an immediate object, and
it can be judged, which leads to shame, but if you live it from the
inside, it is the incarnated subject, a felt and feeling subjectivity—
the sibject, solution to the mind/body problem: the body *is* first
person singular, inhabited, infused, suffused, lit from inside, the
body as instrument, stroked, fingered, pressed, blown into by
the spirit, or the spirit is the body's sound when played by God,
electric, expressive—so the sister and brother feel into knowing,
which is carnal, emotional, spiritual, the knowing sibject knows
another sibject, not an object, all the exclusive dualisms, e.g. subject/
object, girl/boy, good/bad, thought/feeling, concept/intuition fall
away, then God or hermaphrodite is not exclusive: God and/or
hermaphrodite is double aspect, as are what get added to Gregor to
make Gregoire who is Gregor as rebellion, cleverness, knowledge,
but w/o his passivity, instead w/ e as energy or the identity element
in grope theory, and i as identity or the imaginary unit which
comes through creativity, where $i^2 = -1$, but so does $-i^2$. Thus -1 and
27 enter, no, 2.7, don't think about Georg's end, think about how
Gregoire quits eating pseudo-food for thought, goes flat, turns into
a sheet of paper on which Grete/Greta/Gretal can write her score
about her transformed brother Georg, how Georg and Greta in the
expulsion wear sheets of paper not to hide themselves but to print
themselves on book leaves, write with come, so the expulsion is a
pulsing and expression, and the fall is the subjunctive yet true case
of imagination, the sibjunctive, through which they run away from
the shame-filled, no longer creative father and his would-be angelic
sister who are now mere shadows, to be sibjects and live their incest
poetics, incest metaphysics, ergo be *Übergeschwister*, transGods

like the offspring of mercurialism and love, as is Gregoire, who wriggles alongside them, s/he the individual first person singular I-rebellion of Gregor via e, namely the irrational and transcendent constant, which can be raised to the expounding via hyperbolic logorhythm to equal X i.e. ecstatic universal love drug, x i.e. the Eternal Variable, XXX i.e. the sexiest, and Ex, i.e. the expression, Expressionism, Expulsion, aftermath or sense of formerly vs. now, all of this coming about through knowledge of loss and pain, a knowing by intimate acquaintance, i.e. also a feeling, but watchful in always seeing another way of thinking and expressing things, a variation, transposition, thus Gregoire doesn't die but is a sheet of paper that gets blown out the window like a leaf on a breeze, since the sister-in-law left the window open, Georg being downstairs to catch it and write on it, while Greta will follow him out into the world and write, because at the end of the novella, the girl, too, is transformed—

Damnit   just crashed   off my   high

*

More More More / Derangement, Private Pt. 3 (She Performed As the Feminine-Manly True Connection, Was a Hardcore Porn Star) In the '70s of my adolescence *Mädchen* porn! *This cursed sex.*

Snort the white page. *Blow is white* is true iff blow is white. Ditto snow, smack. Blood is black. Snort our lines! *When the end comes in beflecked rooms what if it were spring outside, and a lovely bird sang?*

> Heroin anti-heroine, opium opt out! This is then, that was now.

> The intention is to morpheus yourself. Inhaled him through my savage sisterly nostrils! Oh Georg!

Androgynous ideal: not Grete's hips, rather Greta's hair, like Chopin's. My beautiful brother was my prophet! I walk on water, he went under. He had to die so I could walk on it. He made my body into spirit by grief's transfiguration. *Gray bleeding. Contemplating evil.*

> My brother was my epigraph. I am his grapheme.

Dark spring ways of the pensive.

I played Herodias to his Herod, Salome to his John, he lost his head, proclaimed the incest wrong! All the men did! I am a sexy dancer! Like the biblical tart Salome! Lou Salomé was just a tease while Lulu in that G double-you Bapst flick put out. Whore! Strumpet! Wait, no misogyny! My androgyny is immune to my/their misogyny. But then I became my delicate brother. *If only I could forget his thorn-sting destiny.*

> Can I become Lulu i.e. Loulou in the next book, be the dancing girl and dance away from all this, also from my dancing febrile husband, another prophet or god manqué? The intention is to score another opera, *The Lulu Lays*. So love and sex defeat resentment! My husband said, Quit being jealous! But he himself was fiercely jealous. In his sleep he whined, *Ressentiment.*

> Penis envy? Why? I come not to hold my peace, but to wield my word! *With slender hands picked up a snake.* I am the Prince of Codpiece!

> > This is fucking good cock! I mean coke! Pepsi's in the other book, I am on a Coke diet! Like I did it with Leila back in high school. Talking maniacally, demonically! How you get obsessed with getting more, can't talk about anything else, focus on anything else, once it's all gone.

The Übermess! What will come after my messy godhair gets cut off by *die Lola*! Females are dangerous is misogyny! Or I will be *die Loulou* and do it to myself. Maybe shave my own head with a razor, since I am ready for my brother's war now! *The silent forest.*

But she—namely languishing, lovelorn, seductive: a girl beguiled Gregor Samsa into revealing the secret of his *übermenschlich* strength: his long-wandering Jewishness,

traveling *Seelemenschlichkeit!* Schleppervescence! As
Gregoire, I don't want to be stopped short.

Knowledge of the others' God, His presence in them!

Thrill, horror of knowing your guilt's path of thorns.

I want their words!	I want more words!
Let's do another!	I feel very greedy.

Zarathustra claimed to be only the *Übermensch*'s forerunner, but
Nietzsche danced self-intoxicatedly around his room and called
himself Jesus/Dionysus. I dance around my room and call myself
Loulou Salome/Sally =$_{syn}$ warrior princess of peace—

> *So found the white shape of childhood in the thorn bush,*
> *bleeding toward the cloak of its bridegroom. But he stood*
> *there before her, buried in his steel hair, speechless and*
> *suffering.*

In that one by Hansel Christoph Anders, I had sallied forth, was
wandering in the woods, drenched but fleeing my sad, languid,
irresistibly seductive brother. The princess can't sleep because of P &
~P, opposing propositions.

Why do all the stories crowd into you like an orgy?

They want you to submit to them. They make you spread the
legs of your book and take them and even groan in pleasure.

It isn't forced, it is seduced, i.e. you are. By your own ecstasy,
that drug. Like how you want to rub against, fuck every
thought.

The scholars leave Georg's early, overtly incestuous poems
out of their collections. But I include mine! After all, Adam
and Eve were brother and sister. Dirt and life and death and
dust and corpses and desire—

But, oh, do not think about your rotting brother
while leprosy waxed his forehead silver.
But then you have to think about him.
He went shadow, walked under the fall's stars.
Something fell. *Snow, blue darkness.*

For I was Salome / Herodias and he was Herod / John, and his death
was all my fault. Unless Herod was our father!

*Oh, the bent diffracted deflected declined conjugated appearances of young
women.And the sisters fled in garters to dark gardens with bony old men.*
Not brothers.

Brother!
Brother.

I shouldn't have danced like that. Then he
would never have wanted me.

The Überwench.
The fraternal invert.
The will to unmask yourself.

Are we out of blow already?

*Voice swallowed by God's wind.
Voluptuous death. Children of a dark
race to sex. Nightlike, damned.*

Some fell thing.

*

Garden story. *Deep sleep, mama's white face. Dreck on guilty faces, death,
family tree branches, singing to yourself, playmate, deer, star-faced purity.*

I would like to stop now.

Demons as stories. Associations. Tics. Compulsions.

Torrid syndrome, Turret syndrome, Torrent system, Turing machine.

How our metal is so long too us. But we could leap away
from it. *When father walked away into darkness.*

Greta in her tower of fable—
The Rapunzel fairy tale.
With husband as jailer,
brother as prince.
Sketch of hair.

We liked it when Mademoiselle read us fairy tales, but also
adventure stories; we reenacted them in our garden.

*But the dead man's shadow entered the grieving with crystal steps from
the woods. Stony eyes of the sister, as her madness went to her brother's
brow at the meal, while the mama's suffering hands turned bread to stone.
Silent tongues are silver. Gazing from masks. At twilight, led into the stony
wasteland of the father's dark place by a dead man. Our blood and likeness.
He sank, a rock, into the empty, broken mirror. His sister appeared as a
dying youth, night ate their cursed sex.*

I want to stop now.

I want now to stop.

I cannot live without my lovely, delicate, sad brother.

BROTHER
His wiry tarnished hair

what he inscribed in the adultery book before he left for Vienna:

*Meinem geliebten kleinen Dämon, who has risen from the sweetest
and deepest Märchen aus 1001 Nacht. in memorium! Georg*

That tale of sister and brother love as punishment they're trapped in
a crypt there is no external world and consumed by divine fire burn

to ash gray powder

      the other brothers away
      soon he's leaving her   flaming hair   shirt

If the girl puts him to sleep with her spell or pricks his conscience

      my brother w/ his flask of chloroform, cigarette dipped in
      opium, loitering before the White Angel pharmacy

          could whiteness make you an angel?

scared of Angel Dust in New York in the 1970s then our papa died

    to buy drugs and alcohol, Georg sold his Dostoevsky

        dear brother, we could go underground, be idiots,
        private persons, demons adolescents, brother/sister
        Trakls, punished criminals in our apartment of the
        dead!

When my brother was discharged from the military
he suffered a breakdown wandered tried to resume
at the White Angel but couldn't bear the human
held jobs only for hours days then reenlisted in
the pharmacy at the Innsbruck military hospital and
volunteered for active service end of July medical orderly
for two days tended alone to ninety severely wounded men
fell apart tried to kill himself was prevented   then   not
                                       then   succeeded

        it hurts, to love somebody who is lost
        and you can't help them
        he cried, Rescue me!
        he whispered, You are my salvation!
        and put her into his poems
        but I want to play the piano
        I want to compose songs
        we shared a dope-tipped cigarette

I find your smoking very sexy
also we like to drink too much
it's part of our shared chemistry
how I would soothe him by playing Chopin
or murmuring, Shh, *Liebling*

The only one who understood me is gone

Why didn't you take me with you, my truest brother?

wildness together in Vienna
that stupid florid architecture in Vienna
that day in the park when we were like kids
but our profiles were dark shadows,
Scherenschnitte
our blackness faced the same direction
had the same shape

suicides cannot be buried
Grete vanished into starving
air: *Luftmädchen*
her body went missing

oh please look at the brightness of the day,
its bright gray, even during the warring, the
battles

Is there time for another transformation?   serpentine
swallowing its
own—

he says, Swallow, don't spit out
but jism on her transposed belly
milky, how the pistol shoots

that was later, I mean before

Georg

his languor, despair, his pale skin with dots
his addictions, pessimisms, surrealisms
his beautiful intense imagination, his shocking
images, his sound-stoned words, his stunning
inventions, seductive rhythms, his quiet focus
his dreamy alienation, his social awkwardness
his otherworldly stare, his hot fine gentle fingers
the way his coarse coppery hair stuck up when he
slept, the way he wouldn't leave his room for days
the way he didn't want to work, detested their
superficial values, the way he loved God and beauty
longed for spirituality, tranquility, creativity, could
not bear the ugliness, crassness and violence
outside and inside him
oh dearest brother
I know why it was too much for you
it is too much for me also!

but look: all of that is naked, shameful, unsayable

the world is made of meanings, it's spilling over
with them, they're revolting

why can't it be made purely of sounds?

*

THE TRANSMUTING—IN 26 TRACKS
1 Or awoke to find herself changed into an ung— Ung—. Ungirl,
unGreta? Or double negative, back to the positive except w/ more
complexity, beats. Or their two guns. This pabulum music awful.
Not Schubert, her sonatas! Or his trance. We should return via the
music. The body of the girl. Her fall. Greta too dizzy to stand, exit
her room, join the literary party. Constantly an outsider, wanderer.
If I could say what I really think! 2 The brother Haakon, his gentle
voice. Shouldn't you come out now? Herhis voice in response. Bad
hermaphrodite! Destruction of gender is destruction of sense. It
should be a sound piece. My godpiece. Yes, I am getting up now.
Then the small fist of Wlad. Greta, Greta, what's your problem?
And the sister-in-law, her voice lower than Greta's, Greta, aren't

you well? You seem so thin. Your voice. I am ready, Greta answers,
trying to sound normal. My awkward posture. But unable to stand.
Or unwilling to. 3 The lower part of the body a priority. Pain.
Precisely this lower part of hisher body was at the moment perhaps the
most sensitive. So head first. But fear of falling. The seventh month
already: September. And still I am in a fog. So rock yourself out.
The oscillation, waves. 4 If only they could help. Her father and the
servant-like brother, Gregor. I mean her friend Wlad and her oldest
brother Gregor. The doorbell. Someone from the *Geschlecht.* The sex.
The *Jugend*? Rigid or quivering. Irrational hope that she could open
the door. But Gregor went w/ his light grin and opened it. It was
the head/lead scrivener, writer, who's clerical. 5 It was her dead
brother Georg. Omission of grave. How could she? What is loyalty,
devotion? *So tormented by conscience as to be driven out of herhis mind*
and incapable of leaving their bed. The others innocent, she guilty, so
swing to him. Then fall. Headache. Bruised brow. Something fell,
murmurs the main brother, Georg. Imagine you are Georg, Georg
is you, *One could not really deny that it was possible.* But his leather
military boots. His firm step away. The sister-in-law, Lola, impatient.
Wlad: your room/book is a mess. Georg's wasn't. 6 Greta! Our same
Dämmerung. So called Georg gently, atonally. She's a workaholic now,
says Haakon admiringly. Obsessive work of fretting. Only wants to
cut lines. *Ich komme gleich* could have many meanings. Or unwell.
Impossible, improbably, and Georg says I can use scraps from his
poems. Wlad condescending: ready to come out? Greta: No. A
painful refusal. Silence. The sister-in-law snorts. Has already joined
the others. I would like to be left alone, to rest in pieces. Georg: My
sister, sameslayer, what is wrong? Why don't you come? You have
neglected your duty. Are you stealing more time? 7 But brother, I am
coming now. *A slight illness, an attack of dizziness.* Do not reproach me.
I will be gone by the *n*th month. Please tell God and plead my case to
him. My chest. Banging it on the paragraph. Wish to open the door,
join the ghostly brother. Stand up! But her speech incoherent to them.
I think she's on something again, says the brother. Lola! Get Mlle.
Marlene. Gregor, get *Das Schloss—nein, den Schlüssel.*

8 Now a calm. She unutterable, no longer understandable. Coughs
a bit. Turns the piano key over in herhis mind. Do not remove my
piano. But it was already in the living room, where Lola was learning

to play it. Her hands, fingers small, not long and manly like Greta's. But her charming tone. 9 I cannot make it to the living room. Then your mouth is bleeding. As if a girl w/ her tongue ripped out. But as she reaches the door, opens it, she sees her brother Georg backing away with a sad frown. He's ghostly. Or decomposing, worms in hair, green decay on his skin. Punctuation. 10 The brother Haakon concerned. Greta appears so different when despairing. The pelt of the happy totally different from the pelt of the unhappy. You do not look well. Wlad glances her way, indifferent. 11 Then the window across the street, a gray building: rest cure, mental hospital, asylum. Figures staring: mama, papa? The photo of Georg in military uniform.

12 Greta does not try to speak. This is no comedy. Besides, I've got to escape from my other brothers, my sister. 13 A monologue could be written here. 14 But the chief brother, Georg, backs away, lips parted, shoulders trembling. Secret injunction. Supernatural power. Please don't go yet, dearest brother! 15 There is no other sister, for instance Lola, to charm him to stay, for she has run out to find the governess, assert the governable. 16 Greta moves toward Georg. But Haakon moves in between, stares, transfigured. Georg runs down the stairs. He left behind a pistol, a haircut, a greatcoat. A Gretacoat. 17 Greta grabs the pistol. Will not languish for a whole novella. Too fiercely impatient. Runs back into room, I need another cigarette! 18 Ludvik the cook leaves the scene, horrified. Enter Victor, the cleaner. Greta thinner by the second. But calmer, even peaceful. 19 Gregor returns with the key of G-minor. The party guests are Mo, Leon, and Colin, three charismatic male poets. 20 I think that I will die now. Shoot this scene in the head voice. No, in the chest. 21 My sister-in-law no longer loves me. None of her tenderness. My brother feels repelled despite himself, is distant. My friend disdains me. My dead brother summons me. I was late to work. 22 The *Geschäft — Geschöpf — Erschöpfung*. It is not funny. The photo w/ the spots. She swallowed up by darkness. Animalistic expression on face: hunted animal. 23 Then the tower of meaning clock struck three years later. Twilight. Secret pond. Breathing out last breath, world through their dilated nostrils. 24 Later the brother Victor would come in, find her expired. A book on loan to them, their world, from God. No, from Georg. 25 The suicide note, report? The suicide notes will bear no sense. Will

be pure syntactic sound. The flat dark body? They won't know how to read her marks. 26 It will take them another year just to find her score.

DIE VERSCHOLLENE (MISSING, PRESUMED DEAD, FORGOTTEN)
God withdrew, you go through withdrawal—until you go. *Tzimtzum* = Samson, *Schwester*, sibling. Will my suicide destroy the philistines?

*

SUICIDE ANNOTATIONS TO SURVIVING BROTHERS AND SISTER
Because they are laughing at the party
Because your armpits smell of terror
Because you could not escape from your brother, for even two weeks, much less three years
Because Georg is gone
Because you aren't creating—writing, making music
Because you can't support yourself, stiffen your spine, hold your head high
Because you are no longer worthy of being loved, admired, respected
Because you are disgusting, a wretch
Because I am sick, my mouth hurts, my crotch hurts, I will never be recovered
Because the friends Greta thought she had were mere phantoms
Because the brother who Greta knows has her is her specter
Because to be a spectator, watch only, like her brother Gregor—
Because he can do that in real life, but she, Greta, can't. She plays an instrument
Because to quit being a spectator, seeing. To close the eye that moves from left to right and back, from past to future and back, incessant aspect-shifting
Because to be historical, aggressive and emphatic, with all capital criminal letters
I HAVE TO DO THIS FORGIVE ME
ICH MUSS ES TUN VERZEIHT MIR
Because there is no explanation, only description
Because there is no truth in all the meaning
Because the meanings are jeering in the nightmare
Because *because* is a hollow form, as of life, the world

Because I am my world. Because it's a corpse, but it hurts. Because
its ink is disappearing—

*

SUICIDAL NOTE TO GEORG: REFLECTION OF SIN, HOPE, SUFFERING, THE TRUE
WAY
His cage went in search of a girl. Her page went in search of *einem
Bruder*.

*

GRAPHIC POSTLUDE IN G-MINOR FOR PIANO AND VIOLENCE FROM GRETA
& GEORG (OUR NOTES):

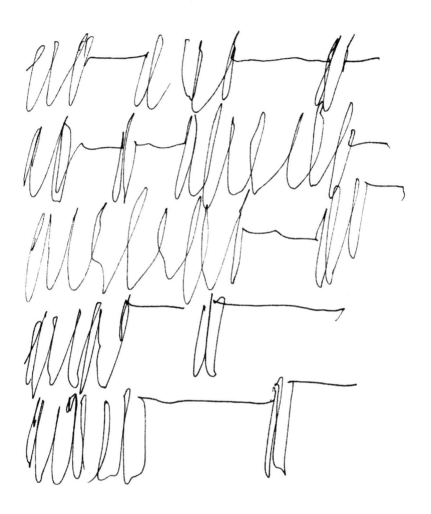

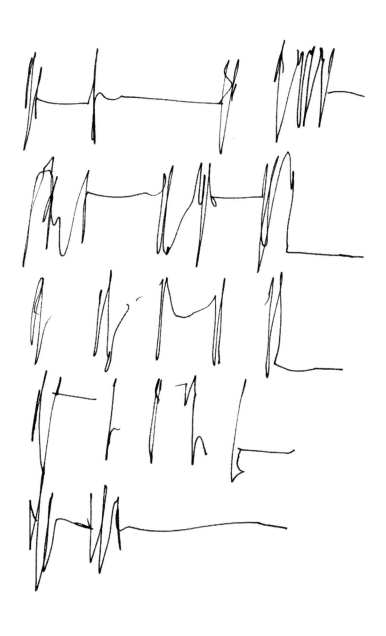

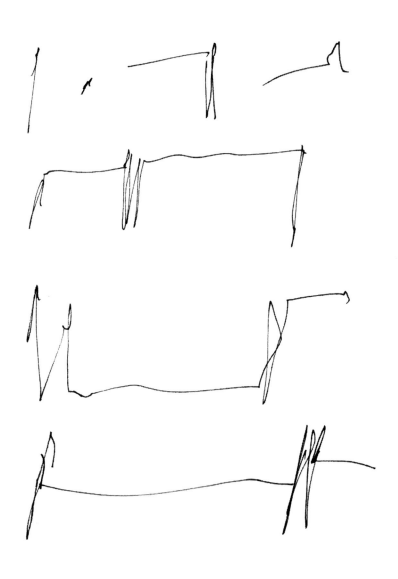

ACKNOWLEDGMENTS

All my thanks/*vielen Dank* to Grete, Georg, Franz, Friedrich, Ludwig, Richard, the siblings Carpenter, the Brothers Grimm, my übereditor Oana, my wunderpublishers Jay and Hazel, my first readers Carla, Erín, and Wayne, my dear, most supportive family and friends (*ua.* Christian, whom I met through our Traklbooks, and Uljana, my German authority), my café crushes, my compelling city. My gratitude to the editors of the following presses for publishing excerpts from *Metaphysical Licks: Aufgabe, BOMB, Boog City Reader, Fence, Mrs. Maybe, Try!, The Recluse.*

This book is dedicated to Odile.

BACKGROUND READINGS

Trakl, Georg, tr. Alexander Stillmark, *Poems and Prose, A Bilingual Edition,* Northwestern University Press: Evanston, 2005.

Trakl, Georg, tr. Daniel Simko, *Autumn Sonata, Selected Poems of Georg Trakl,* Asphodel Press/Moyer Bell: Wakefield, 1998.

Basil, Otto, *Georg Trakl, in Selbstzeugnissen und Bilddokumenten,* Rowolt: Reinbeck bei Hamburg, 1965.

Chiu, Charles S., Edith Borchardt, tr., *Women in the Shadows, Mileva Einstein-Maríc, Margarete Jeanne Trakl, Lise Meitner, Milena Jesenská, and Margarete Schütte-Lihotzky,* Peter Lang: New York, 2008.

Detsch, Richard, *Georg Trakl's Poetry: Toward a Union of Opposites,* Pennsylvania State Press: University Park, 1983.

Graziano, Frank, ed., *Georg Trakl: A Profile,* Logbridge-Rhodes: Durango, 1983.

Sharp, Francis Michael, *The Poet's Madness: A Reading of Georg Trakl,* Cornell University Press: Ithaca, 1981.

Wagner, Richard, *Tristan & Isolde (English National Opera Guides: 6),* John Calder Ltd., London/Riverrun Press: New York, 1981.

Weichselbaum, Hans, *Georg Trakl: Bildmonographie,* Müller: Salzburg-Wien, 1994.

Williams, Eric, *The Mirror & The Word, Modernism, Literary Theory & Georg Trakl,* University of Nebraska Press: Lincoln, 1993.

COLOPHON
First Edition, fall 2014
Distributed in Canada by the Literary Press Group www.lpg.ca
Distributed in the US by Small Press Distribution www.spdbooks.org
Shop on-line at www.bookthug.ca

BOOK
PRODUCTION
WAR ECONOMY
STANDARD

Cover art by Gregoire Pam Dick
Cover design by Gregoire Pam Dick and Jay MillAr
Type by Jay MillAr and Gregoire Pam Dick
Copy edited by Ruth Zuchter

Gregoire Pam Dick (aka Mina Pam Dick, Jake Pam Dick, et al.) is the author
of *Delinquent* (Futurepoem, 2009). Her writing has appeared in *BOMB, frieze,
The Brooklyn Rail, Aufgabe, EOAGH, Fence, Matrix, Open Letter, Poetry Is Dead,*
and elsewhere, and has been featured in *Postmodern Culture*; it is included
in the anthologies *The Sonnets* (ed. S. Cohen and P. Legault, Telephone,
2012) and *Troubling the Line: Trans and Genderqueer Poetry and Poetics,* (ed. TC
Tolbert and Tim Trace Peterson, Nightboat, 2013). Her philosophical work
has appeared in a collection published by the International Wittgenstein
Symposium. Also an artist and translator, Dick lives in New York City, where
she is currently doing work that makes out and off with Büchner, Wedekind,
Walser, and Michaux.